ANCESTRAL LINES

ANCESTRAL LINES

Culture & Identity in the Work
of
Six Contemporary Poets

Linden Peach

U.S. DISTRIBUTOR
DUFOUR EDITIONS
CHESTER SPRINGS,
PA 19425-0449
(215) 458-5005

SEREN

SEREN BOOKS is the book imprint of
Poetry Wales Press Ltd
Andmar House, Tondu Road, Bridgend, Mid Glamorgan

© Linden Peach

The publisher acknowledges the financial support of the
Welsh Arts Council

Printed in Palatino by WBC Print Ltd, Bridgend

CONTENTS

ACKNOWLEDGEMENTS

Acknowledgements are due to Peters, Fraser & Dunlop Ltd for permission to quote from Tony Harrison; to Faber & Faber to quote from Oliver Reynolds and Douglas Dunn; Carcanet to quote from Gillian Clarke.

Introduction

Some of our most exciting poetry is being written away from the economic and cultural centre, at the social and geographical margins, where a great weight of historical experience is being reclaimed and identities are being reaffirmed. Yet this phenomenon — the implications of which constitute the subject of this book — has only been partly recognised by critics and then usually tangled with over simplistic notions of how the poetry re-creates the past.

The emphasis of this book is upon the way in which poets writing geographically or socially outside the English middle-class tradition seek to define their identity in relation to the history — political, social and familial — of their own cultural context. Poetry, of course, is judged foremost upon its language so in order to do the poets justice the book eschews a comprehensive survey in favour of a detailed study of selected representative writing. It is an approach, however, which highlights the complex issues involved in their work and in this area of study.

What makes this poetry especially complex is that it not only brings particular pasts to our attention but undertakes a reassessment of them. Often this means challenging preconceptions which the reader might be expected to hold. The latter is often presumed to be an outsider who has to be drawn into an involvement not only with the past but, also, as we shall see, with issues arising out of such an engagement.

It is misleading to think in simple terms of a re-created past, for the educated writers themselves often exist in a strained relationship with their pre-literate ancestries. There is often friction between the text as an acceptable mode of communication in the socio-cultural mainstream and the 'structure of feeling', to use Raymond Williams' phrase, within the community from have frequently overlooked the fact that if that past were as fully accessible to, and capable of being inhabited by the writer as the critics would like to suggest, the poetry would not have been written!

The book argues that their works cannot be discussed adequately without reference to the issues of culture and identity which they raise. Thus, the question as to whether it is possible even to think in terms of an Irish identity per se or whether we can only think in terms of two Irish communities must inform any discussion of Heaney's work. The work of Gillian Clarke and Oliver Reynolds cannot be considered without acknowledging that in Wales there are two cultures: a rural-orientated Welsh-language culture in North and West Wales and an industrial-orientated, English-language culture in the South.

The texts selected for detailed consideration challenge conventional and static, even outworn, notions of what it is to be Welsh, Irish, Northern and/or working-class. Throughout, the focus is upon how the poetry emerges from authentic engagements with the realities of life in these countries and regions and from each poet's sense of complex personal, regional and national identities.

Moreover, in pursuing general issues arising from the socio-economic processes of colonisation, marginalisation and regionalisation clichéd references to crises of identity, form, language or structure have been avoided. Every worthwhile writer and every period we might care to mention bring at least some, if not all, of these into question. But, in examining the work of many contemporary poets, it is impossible to ignore their realisation of how numerous post-1960's social movements have attached themselves to new, emergent identities and, in the work of Harrison and Dunn, for example, how traditional 'objective' identities such as class are losing their privileged positions in favour of identities constructed around new images — market styles, consumer culture.

Of course, the word 'culture' itself is ambivalent and contentious. Much of the controversy has focused upon its connotations of superiority and refinement, the implicit and explicit distinctions between 'high' and 'popular' culture, and the way in which culture can be, and often is, commodified as a form of capital — possession of which often legitimises the dominance of one class, social sector or ethnic group over another. Thanks to semiotics, structuralism, narratology and theories of discourse, the very concept of fixed positions which any culture might seek to secure has become redundant. Recent linguistic and anthropological theories have provided us with an appreciation of culture as a process in which individuals and groups define themselves within larger sign systems and it is this concept which underpins the discussion of much of the poetry.

As explained earlier in this introduction, the core of the book is a close reading of work by significant, representative poets. Three aspects of working outside the English, middle-class tradition, at the social and geographical margins, are considered. There is a particular emphasis upon culture and identity in relation to ideas of nationhood, ideas pursued here with reference to Irish and Welsh poets, but applicable to writers from, say, Scotland. Irish and Welsh cultures have sustained particular gender stereotypes and the book discusses concepts of identity in relation to gender, a discussion extended to writers with a working-class ancestry from the North of England. Writers from this region have been selected because they are marginalised both socially and geographically and, therefore, present especially interesting case studies, but obviously much of what is said is applicable to writers of working-class origins from other areas. Douglas Dunn has been included not as a Scottish poet — although, as we acknowledge, his Scottish origins are not irrelevant to his poetry or this study — but because he is an interesting contrast to Tony Harrison, who, unlike Dunn, writes about his working-class ancestry from the inside, as it were, and because he is the first poet to write in detail about the changing nature of working-class culture and the way in which identities are being increasingly constructed around new signs and images. Of course, the concepts of culture and identity in the work of particular writers cannot be discussed in relation to nationhood, region, gender and class in isolation from each other and the book has sought to avoid such false distinctions. The problematic nature of these concepts is acknowledged, but the emphasis is upon the poetry and how identity in relation to these concepts is complex and problematic for the individual concerned in order to allow as much room as possible for a discussion of the poetry as poetry. The book is rooted in the conviction that readers come to the works of these poets not for information and wisdom about identity and culture in the abstract, but first and foremost for the experience of the poetry.

It cannot be denied, however, that many critics and writers working at the social and geographical margins have also been eloquent in debates about the myths of nationhood, have been involved in developing politicised concepts of history and in reflecting upon the potential tensions between poetry as art and their own concern to provide a public platform for larger issues around notions of culture, hegemony and identity. The introductory chapters of this book review the particular slant given to these issues by scholars and critics working themselves at the geographical and social margins. The purpose of these chapters is, then, not only to provide an academic framework for the book, but to acknowledge the particular and sometimes idiosyncratic way in which these issues are viewed at the margins. However, it is also agreed that the poetry betrays the need for greater recognition of the problematic nature of the relationship between the individual and his/her cultural origins than some recent theoretical work tends to admit.

There is much talk nowadays about growing cultural uniformity throughout Britain.... But the talk is often vitiated by being an expression of the condition it ostensibly deplores, when it shows complete ignorance of the degree to which cultural, regional and local differences still affect many people's sense of themselves.

Jeremy Hooker (*Poetry of Place*)

PART ONE

ISSUES AND PERSPECTIVES
AT THE MARGINS

CHAPTER ONE

POLITICS AND MYTH IN WALES
AND IRELAND

The wintry haw is burning out of season,
crab of the thorn, a small light for small people,
wanting no more from them but that they keep
the wick of self-respect from dying out,
not having to blind them with illumination.

Seamus Heaney ('The Haw Lantern')

I

In the process of learning a language, we absorb the myths and forms which influence, regulate and control our social evolution. The language, and ultimately the myths and forms, which we enter in a Lacanian sense offer us a refuge from isolation. They provide us with a framework within which to achieve orientation and definition. But as, for example, Tony Harrison found in the working-class culture in which he grew up, and Welsh women writers have found in traditionally male-orientated Welsh culture, this framework is often problematic and often involves conflict. Many of the theoretical writings on myth, history and culture originating from the geographical and social margins are disappointingly vague on the problematic nature of this framework. As Gareth Stedman Jones has pointed out, there began around 1956 an "unfreezing of historical debate" in Britain.[1] The practice of history itself came under a critical scrutiny which eventually led to the identification of two models of literary and cultural history: a progressive model which stressed development and continuity and a model that concentrated on myth, symbol, paradox, ambiguity and irony.[2]

For many writers working from positions outside the conventional parameters of cultural power, it is this latter model which, as we shall see, has become increasingly significant. From this time also dates our awareness that literary history involves works of the historical past and a consciousness of history. That it is not enough to relate historical concepts to *le signifie*: that to write history is to make history and to be made by history.

In cultural studies from Wales, Ireland and Scotland, as in other colonies, there is often, unsurprisingly, an emphasis upon a developing sense of nationhood and the way in which this has been concomitant with the construction of mythical, idealised pasts. Exploring the long-standing connection between poetry, history and myth in Wales, in what he has described as "the Taliesin tradition", Emyr Humphreys, for example, argues: "The function of praise poetry in the Celtic world was to celebrate and sustain the social order. In the Welsh context, from the very beginning, this also involved the poet as the voice of resistance, the tireless mouthpiece of the endless process of defending a realm under siege."[3] But many of these accounts fail to acknowledge the full complexity of mythical frameworks.

The Irish scholar, Kevin Nolan, in 'Ancient Myth and Poetry' puts his finger on the nub when he describes how nineteenth-century nationalism "was the way in which the medium of poetry, of verse at least, was used to propagate a concept of society, a concept of history, a concept of a collective memory".[4] Nolan's work is more complex than Humphreys' thesis because he recognises that "a sense of confidence that the history of the past could justify a distinctive nationality in the present"[5] which emerged in nineteenth-century Ireland was postulated through myth in the Barthes sense, as a mode of signification.

Prys Morgan, a Welsh scholar, also approaches national identity from this perspective. His study of how Welsh identity was forged in the nineteenth century highlights attempts to view the landscape as numinous; the creation of a "heraldry of culture" and "a complex of symbols and signs standing for Wales"; ballads on romantic themes; and the celebration of Welsh heroes.[6] It was in the nineteenth century, for example, that the Welsh woman in her *pais* and *betgwn* became accepted as the symbol *par excellence* of Wales and the Welsh national anthem was launched.

But in Wales, Prys Morgan's approach is not yet commonplace. It is only Ireland has provided an entrenched understanding of the political dimension of myth-making as a mode of signification, encapsulated in Lady Augusta Gregory's term for the phenomenon, 'image-making, which has ironically become a buzz-word of the 1980s and 1990s. Appropriately, her first publication was a collection of essays by Ireland's 'image-makers', the strong people whose dream was love of country. It demonstrates how she understood that only when myth has become a form, can it serve an historical purpose:

> I had from the beginning a vision of historical plays being sent by us through all the counties of Ireland. For to have a real success and to come into the life of the country, one must touch a real and eternal emotion, and history comes only next to religion in our country .... I still hope to see a little season given up every year to plays on history and a sequence at the Abbey ....[7]

It is this understanding which separates her work from that of Emyr Humphreys even though her argument, on one level, is similar to that of Emyr Humphreys that, even in the twentieth century, "myth-making" is "a most potent weapon in the struggle for survival" as "the thread" which connects sensitive young people to "an honourable past".[8]

The use of the phrase "an honourable past" is enough to suggest the unproblematic way in which mythical frameworks are often perceived. Both Lady Gregory and Emyr Humphreys stress how myths of an idealised past provide status and a sense of continuity for the Celtic colonies. In fact, during the period 1880-1940, Irish literature in English made "a fetish of continuity". As Seamus Deane argues, continuity was "an enabling instrument, a kind of legal fiction which proposed the idea of an Irish social contract as the basis for the belief in the existence of a specifically Irish civilization."[9] It is underpinned, as Deane stresses, by "a fascinating theory of history of the kind which we readily encounter in Romantic aesthetics" i.e. of history being an engagement with the fortunes of the imagination:

> the dream of an evolutionary continuity in a civilization which fetches its origins from some misty past is also a characteristic of the conservative politics which the main line of European Romanticism has always held in considerable affection.[10]

Of course, romanticising the Celtic past is a European phenomenon, a late eighteenth and early nineteenth-century reaction against eighteenth-century polemics. But it involves a simplistic way of looking at Celtic countries which has survived into the twentieth century and in cinema this traditional view of myth has become interestingly fused with the more modern view of myth as form. As far as Ireland is concerned, this fusion is epitomised in Ford's film *The Quiet Man* (1953) made in the wake of the Second World War and in the midst of the Korean War. In the film Sean Thornton, a rich and guilty retired fighter, escapes his guilt, which is representative of the guilt of post Second World War America, by moving to Innisfree and by exchanging sword for ploughshare, as it were. We follow Sean through a process of demechanisation — he arrives by train, takes a carriage, a bicycle, a horse and, finally, ends up walking — until he is able to be accommodated to the rural (mythical) Ireland.[11] The power of the image of an idealised past can be seen also in John Ford's adaptation of Richard Llewellyn's novel, *How Green Was My Valley*. It is set, as Peter Stead has said, "in a mythical Shangri-La which is part Irish, part North Walian but mostly just the land of nursery rhymes and whatever real Welshness the film has is contributed by just one actor [Rhys Williams] and by a choir."[12] It is, of course, schmaltz, but it does depict myths of family and community in an idealised Wales to which even twentieth-century audiences responded.

II

Among many scholars working at the social and geographical margins, there has been considerable debate around the issues of continuity, traditional Welshness and traditional Irishness of a kind which it would be difficult to imagine happening elsewhere. It is as necessary to acknowledge this, in discussing writers working outside the conventional parameters of cultural power, as it is to acknowledge their interest in the problematic nature of the mythical framework to which language in the Lacanian sense admits us.

In Irish literature, the great demythologizer is Patrick Kavanagh "who repudiated the very idea of the Irish Revival and with that, all its rhetoric of power, suasion and possession."[13]

His fidelity to the contours of rural Irish life has brought him much criticism from Seamus Heaney who has lamented how: "The 'matter of Ireland', mythical, historical or literary, forms no significant part of his material." While Deane sympathises with Kavanagh and, also, with Montague, seeing them as signifying the emergence of modern Ireland out of the heroic pastoral past,[14] Heaney has grave doubts which he expresses in 'From Monaghan to the Grand Canal' (1975): "Without myth, without masters, 'no system, no plan', he lived from hand to mouth and unceremoniously where Yeats — and Sidney — fed deliberately and ritually, in the heart's rag-and-bone shop." But in expanding upon this comparison of Yeats and Kavanagh in 'The Sense of Place', Heaney is forced to acknowledge a crucial irony: Kavanagh gave "the majority of the Irish people, for whom the experience of life on the land was perhaps the most formative, an image of themselves that nourished their sense of themselves in that serious way which Synge talked about in his preface."

A similar debate between the mythologizers and the demythologizers has occurred in Wales. The Welsh historian, Gwyn A. Williams, like Seamus Heaney, acknowledges how Yeats "immersed himself in the history and the mythology of the people to whom he belonged and whom he wished to serve by remaking them..."[15] But Williams emphasises Yeats' eventual decision to walk "naked" out of this mythology. He argues that there is as much continuity in the history of the actual people of Wales as has been constructed by, for example, "the Taliesin tradition".

The way in which the problematic nature of this "fetish of continuity" has given the discussion of myth in Wales, as in Ireland, a special slant is evident in one of Jeremy Hooker's essays. In his study of five of what he calls 'Anglo-Welsh' poets, he sets Gwyn A. Williams' argument that myth has only served to obscure a vital historical reality against Humphreys' insistence upon the importance of mythology for Wales.[16] The epigraph to Williams' *When Was Wales?* is a poem by R.S. Thomas, 'Welsh History', which, Hooker reminds us, Williams claims sanctifies "a monstrous historical lie".[17] Neither Hooker nor Williams could have known that 'Welsh History' would be chosen by R.S. Thomas to open his *Welsh Airs* (1987), a collection is an appropriate poem with which to begin *Welsh Airs* because it acknowledges in the first verse the importance of mythopoeia in the Welsh cultural heritage. The first verse celebrates the way in which the Welsh chieftains kept the English at bay in the hills and created islands of Welshness which the invaders could not penetrate. Yet the poem is ambivalent. Thomas knows that it was not quite like this. He knows that there was a great deal of complicity, that not all Welshmen joined the battle for survival, that some joined with the English and that not even all of those who fought the English had the interests of, or even a sense of, the Welsh nation uppermost in their minds. This particular poem goes on to tell of complicity and treason, of years wasted in the service of English masters.

It is a significant poem because it not only acknowledges the importance of the traditional view of myth in Welsh culture, but approaches myth as problematic. Thomas leaves us in no doubt as to the fact that what is commonly thought of as the Welsh cultural heritage is a construction, an idealisation of the past. In the last verse, the awareness of the past, of the importance of myth, is even opposed to Thomas' now famous indictment of the Welsh as an introspective, narrow-minded people too obsessed with "gnawing the bones / Of a dead culture". But as Prys Morgan reminds us: "in order to succeed a lie must be a half-truth or a white lie, that is to say, the images, myths and clichés which have the most powerful effect are made up in part from real elements, although adorned with imagination."[19]

As we consider the poetry written at the social and geographical margins, the extent of the problematic nature of the mythical frameworks in which the writers are working will become increasingly clear. Up until now, critics have discussed the problematic nature of this mythical framework in Wales mainly in relation to the myth of rural Wales. The poet, John Tripp, complained in an interview:

> rural themes were always thought to be more 'poetic' than urban ones, set among the aerials and housing estates. The pastoral has had a fatal attraction for many Welsh poets, to the exclusion of all else just as the clichés of pit and chapel have maimed other poets. I prefer a landscape with figures, on the whole.[20]

If Welsh literature in English has seemed to overstress the

rural at the expense of the urban, this impression is due in no small part to the dominance and the influence of R.S. Thomas. Indeed, there are a number of writers who have avoided traditional Welshness and have written from knowledge of regional, urban, English-speaking Wales. It was against this trend that R.S. Thomas set his own work, declaring in 'Llenyddiaeth Eingl-Gymreig' (1952):

> But to me, the true Wales is still to be found in the country. The heavy industries came from outside and are something new: but the country tradition runs back across the centuries as something essentially Welsh, and every Welsh writer whatever his language, has a responsibility in this respect.

Unlike R.S. Thomas, Gwyn A. Williams sees rural Wales as a problematic myth which means little to the people of industrial Wales and which is bound up with a larger, equally problematic myth: the *gwerin*. As it developed in the late nineteenth century, the essential characteristics of the *gwerin* pointed to a cultured, educated, responsible, self-disciplined, respectable, but genial poor. They were "Welsh-speaking, Nonconformist, imbued with the more social virtues of Dissent, bred on the Bible and good practice."[22] The concept of the *gwerin* ignores other possible perspectives on small, close-knit communities — such as those taken by Caradoc Evans, for example — and also the realities of industrial Wales. Yet, in some respects, it has become part-and-parcel of Welsh national identity.

The industrial, Welsh working classes are the counterpoint to this myth. Gwyn A. Williams' explanation for the transition of urban areas from Welsh-speaking to English-speaking stresses the importance of the way in which the Welsh language and a mythical Wales, remote from the realities of urban industrial life, were perceived as synonymous: the fact that the Welsh language was "the language of the chapel, of political interests which seemed irrelevant, of a rather meagre recent literature which did not connect"; and the fact that English was "the language of militancy, self-assertion and rejection of servility" while Welsh was the language of "conservatism and accommodation".[23]

We must, however, place Gwyn A. Williams' arguments in a larger context for they are underpinned by considerable doubt that Wales has a future which will continue any degree of Welshness from the past.[24] His vision of twenty-first century Wales is a nightmare:

> ...a Costa Bureaucratica in the south and a Costa Geriatrica in the north; in between sheep, holiday homes burning merrily away and fifty folk museums where there used to be communities.[25]

But Williams is one of the few Welsh writers to acknowledge the full problematic extent of the way in which Wales, in a time of cultural crisis, has turned increasingly to the past:

> This recovered tradition is increasingly operating in terms of a Celebration of a Heroic Past which seems rarely to be brought to bear on vulgarly contemporary problems.... This is not to encapsulate a past, it is to sterilize it. It is not to cultivate an historical consciousness; it is to eliminate it.[26]

III

Few Welsh readers will need reminding that the mythical framework in which Welsh writers work and try to achieve orientation and definition is made problematic by the relative status of the Welsh and English languages. But once again the arguments have been conducted along lines which have made them increasingly irrelevant to younger Welsh poets even though some of the underlying issues are still important. Gwyn A. Williams finds in Wales an increasing mutual alienation of Welsh-speaking and English-speaking Welsh people.[27] While his picture is too generalized to be an accurate account of what is happening in every area of Wales, the English-language Welsh have tended to accept "the seniority and organic continuity of Welsh-language literature." There are three factors behind this:

> the emergence in the post-war period of a new Welsh-speaking middle class, served by its own intelligentsia and promoting itself through ethnic solidarity, of which literature constituted a major component; a coherent ideology, borrowed variously from English Romanticism, cultural anthropology and elements of a perceived Welsh tradition, again primarily literary in orientation; and finally

the reproduction of this class and its ideology through new institutions and education.[29]

So many of even the most supportive claims for English-language Welsh literature betray a fundamental insecurity vis-à-vis the Welsh language in Wales. Raymond Garlick in an often quoted description saw what he called the "Anglo-Welsh" as "at one remove". Even the view that R.S. Thomas defended the Welsh language and the Welsh nation and made a positive contribution to the promotion of Welsh cultural identity by bringing issues to an English-language audience seems like an apology for the fact that he did not write in the Welsh language.

Welsh, English-language essays on this subject have slanted the debate in the direction of R.S. Thomas' work. Of course, in R.S. Thomas' poetry all the negative dimensions of being what he calls "Anglo-Welsh" are stressed. They have been often referred to and are conveniently summarised by J.P. Ward: "his utter disgust at his own people; his anguish at his own ignorance (for poetic purposes) of the Welsh language; and his curious orientation to the invading stranger and culture."[30] They are sentiments taken to extremes in *What is a Welshman?* which Ward has described as one of the most "negative and nihilistic" of Thomas' collections of poetry.[31]

Unfortunately, the particular slant given to discussion of the rôle and status of English-language Welsh writers in Wales by this emphasis on R.S. Thomas' work is not readily applicable to many younger Welsh poets. R.S. Thomas felt himself estranged from what he regarded as the real Wales, Welsh-speaking Wales, through cultural circumstances and familial origins.

Unable to write adequately in Welsh, he felt himself, as a poet committed to his art, compelled (even banished) to become only an English-language, Welsh writer. Indeed, he blamed his parents for not having brought him up in a Welsh-language culture, recognising that, generally speaking, only a Welsh person of Welsh-speaking parents is likely to become an able Welsh-language poet. In 1964, he declared bitterly that he would live next door to a slut so long as she "can speak Welsh / And bear children / To accuse the womb / That bore me." Undoubtedly, as Ward suggests, there are strong psychic thrusts to Thomas' nationalism![32] Brian Morris has also drawn attention to the sense of alienation that accompanied him, even in Manafon:

> The people of Manafon habitually speak English, not Welsh, and in their social and political life they look as much towards the English towns of Oswestry and Hereford as to the local Welsh market-towns of Y Trallwng (Welshpool) and Y Drenewydd (Newtown).[33]

On a profounder level, however, R.S. Thomas' work is relevant to contemporary discussions of culture and identity in Wales. His poetry has proved important for the English-speaking, Welsh intelligentsia because it has enabled them to define and assume a national identity, albeit one subordinate to that enjoyed by the Welsh-speaking intelligentsia.

Moreover, it was with the work of R.S. Thomas, or rather a small section of it, as Tony Bianchi points out, that an English-speaking readership in Wales was able "to recognise itself as a specific and corporate readership".[34] While earlier English-language, Welsh writers, such as Dylan Thomas, won many readers, they failed to create a coherent readership. Through a core of R.S. Thomas' work, however, an English-speaking readership could engage in a discourse from which it had been historically excluded.[35]

In the end, it must be admitted, this proved unsatisfactory. For, as Bianchi argues, the English-language readers were engaged in a discourse about culture and identity in Wales only to be excluded again. Many of the poems, Bianchi reminds us, associate the reader with a number of negatively inscribed positions — exile, outsider, the machine, the public, England — from which (s)he is enticed into accepting alternative values: nature, Wales, history.[36] But Bianchi suggests that "the reader's removal from one set of values to the other is either incomplete or impossible to achieve." Ultimately, "no intelligentsia organically related to a broad English-speaking constituency can create itself within the terms of the dominant literary discourse."[37]

J.P. Ward has identified two categories of nationalist poem in R.S. Thomas' work: "In one sense only a few of Thomas's poems are fully nationalist in the sense of facing the oppressor or enemy, or overtly declaring a political intention. In another sense they all are, and we have then to decide what is the relation between the direct ones and the more oblique..."[38] The

classification could be extended beyond R.S. Thomas to all contemporary poetry in Wales. The work of many of the poets we
shall consider — because of their place at the social and geographical margins — is highly politicised. In a later chapter, we
shall explore the nature of this politicisation in the work of
some specific writers. In each case, we shall see that the politicisation involves a quarrel with the cultural framework in which
they work and that their relationships with the past are more
complex than we have been led to expect.

A number of critics believe that poetry and politics are not
comfortable bed-fellows. As Ward has pointed out, R.S. Thomas
himself suggested in 1961 that poetry has such subtle, unex-
pected and immediate origins that it is difficult to talk of "nationalist poetry" in the sense of a defiant and deliberate call to
action.[39] It is a view that has been argued more recently by Greg
Hill who employs Geoffrey Hill's distinction between writers
who deal with "dark disputed matter" and those who "push on
pragmatically with the matter in hand."[40] John Barnie, too, has
urged writers to avoid politics and to write only under the influence of creative surges.[41] In the essay on five contemporary
English-language Welsh poets to which we referred earlier,
Jeremy Hooker has similarly cautioned, in discussing the work
of Mike Jenkins: "Overconfidence makes his writing flat and
crude, and his caricature, of opponents or attitudes, are the
poetic equivalent of slogans. The real history is always more
interesting, and the history which he really cares about, the history of working people, he treats with much more verbal subtle-
ty, richness, and force."[42] John Tripp admitted:

> ...but there's always the danger when dealing with political or
> social themes that you can easily lose control. The end-product can
> come across as bluster, posturing or discursiveness.[43]

We find the same concern with poetry and politics among
Irish critics and once again there are many who feel the two do
not mix easily. Edna Longley has declared:

> Poetry and politics, like church and state, should be separated. And
> for the same reasons: mysteries distort the rational processes which
> ideally prevail in social relations; while ideologies confiscate the
> poetry's special passport to *terra incognita*.[44]

In support of her argument she invokes Yeats and, from more recent times, Conor Cruise O'Brien, who called "the area where literature and politics overlap" an "unhealthy intersection".

Despite these reservations, the politics and the poetry are compatible in the work of the writers we shall discuss because the poetry is at least partly rooted in, and inspired by, their own awareness of themselves outside the conventional parameters of cultural power and by their awareness of the problematic nature of the cultural framework in which they write. In entering the debate, Mike Jenkins himself, while admitting that didactic political poetry can be ineffective, advises that political poetry comes in many forms and guises. Citing Jeremy Hooker's argument that more poets now in Wales seem to be concerned with the issues of today and are writing out of the communities in which they live, Jenkins argues, some might say from naive faith in human nature, that political poetry in Wales has not been "a question of theories, but of the people and their fundamental goodness."[45]

In setting poetry about theories and poetry about people in opposition to each other, Jenkins anticipates Robert Minhinnick's assessment of Raymond Garlick's work. Garlick shares with R.S. Thomas a bitter disappointment with the Welsh people. In Minhinnick's view, Garlick encourages us to see himself as an over-severe schoolmaster:

> And the people who fail in his classes are the great majority of the Welsh nation who pay no real heed to the language issue. Instead, they carry on with their lives as if nothing fundamentally important was happening when the protestors are gaoled or fined and the police move in to break up a sit-in demonstration. These apathetic, incurious, politically purblind or other-wise occupied legends get extremely low marks from the poet.[46]

While Minhinnick admits the importance of Garlick's blood-and-guts style of writing, he argues that "the hard-nosed, full-frontal nationalism of the writers of the sixties" was taken as far as possible by Garlick and his contemporaries such as Tripp and Stephens and that Garlick's Wales "is difficult to discover because it is unpeopled". While there are portraits of old ladies, Minhinnick looks "in vain for an interest in the population of this country he is so concerned about". In placing this criticism within the context of a larger argument about poetry and nationalism, he employs the same kind of antithesis which we find in R.S. Thomas himself, Greg Hill, John Barnie and Jeremy Hooker: "Problems for 'nationalist' poets occur when they seek to make statements about whole countries or great movements of people. Poetry lives largely in particular not generalized detail."[47]

Since the 1960s, then, views have emerged of the English-language Welsh as riddled with guilt and insecurity, as accepting their estrangements and as failing to challenge their seeming inferiority to the Welsh-language intelligentsia. English-language, Welsh poetry is seen as presided over by a poet who engages an English readership only to exclude it, while poetry and nationalism are seen by many writers as mixing as well as oil and water. As we shall see later, however, the concerns of younger poets with the problematic cultural framework in which they seek orientation and definition are such that many of the arguments which have been developed around R.S. Thomas' work seem increasingly irrelevant and in their work the poetry and politics are compatible and inseparable.

We shall also see that a number of poets writing in the English language are producing work which may not be overtly political, but whose aesthetic, as Tony Curtis has said of Gillian Clarke, is "heavily weighed by passionate convictions regarding Wales, and pre-supposes such feelings in her audience".[49] They do not display the tub thumping we associate with Garlick and Tripp nor do they carry the same deep-rooted estrangement of R.S. Thomas. Although they may feel the pangs of exclusion from Welsh-language Wales on one level, they feel strong bonds of affinity with it on another. Their aesthetic is so Welsh, despite the fact that they write in English, that it is more profitable and illuminating to focus upon what is un-English in their work rather than upon what is not Welsh. Ultimately, the former leads us back to Wales.

This has proved a successful way of approaching the work of Dylan Thomas, as Walford Davies has demonstrated, because arguing that Thomas' work is Welsh is beset by problems. Although both Thomas' parents came from Welsh, working-class families, his father, a university-educated teacher of English in Swansea Grammar School, prevented Thomas himself from learning Welsh and even sent him to elocution lessons so that he would not speak English with a Welsh accent! Thomas himself, born and brought up in an anglicised suburb of Swansea, could champion his Welshness and also go to great lengths — especially in the early years — to deny it, displaying a deep-seated hatred of his homeland and its people. Yet he was not isolated from the Welsh language: his mother was Welsh-speaking and the relatives with whom he spent many holidays spoke Welsh routinely and regularly. His father, too, was a Welsh-speaker and taught Welsh at evening classes for extra income to help maintain their seemingly middle-class life style. Thomas was aware of the Welsh language and that the people of Swansea spoke English in a way that was un-English.[50] Walford Davies has demonstrated through an account of the un-English way Thomas uses English that Welsh culture pervades his art.[51] Just as the way the middle-class Uplands failed to separate Thomas completely from a working-class culture — present through his own mother and her friends and relatives, some of his school friends and the excursions he made into the less salubrious parts of Swansea — his father failed to isolate him from the Welsh language.

That we should pay more attention to the positive connections between Wales and the English-language speaker is the linchpin of a less divisive approach to the whole issue of the existence of Welsh-language and English-language speakers in Wales. Mike Jenkins has argued:

> A poet cannot be separated (even in the case of a Proust Mark II!) from the daily concerns of the folk around. This is especially true of Wales, where our writers (in both languages) have rarely worked in isolation and have so often articulated the thoughts and emotions of the victims of exploitation. Drama, fiction and poetry all have ears for the language of the streets, which, even if it is English, will in most cases have been powerfully influenced by Welsh either in its vocabulary and/or intonations.[52]

Mike Jenkins is, of course, one of the younger generation of English-language Welsh poets who came to prominence in the 1980s and who "developing from the example of Glyn Jones and Idris Davies, are extending their concern deep into urban and industrial areas of English-speaking Wales".[53] While this means "writing from where they are, or where they come from, not only from their social circumstances but from their lives and their parents' lives", Hooker acknowledges the fear of some critics "that they [might] lose all specific Welshness".[58] In a sense, Jenkins in the passage quoted above is answering this fear. For the new, English-language, Welsh, urban poets are redefining the way we regard the interrelationships between nationalism, culture, ancestry and identity.

CHAPTER TWO

THE BURDEN OF HISTORY: NORTHERN ENGLAND, WALES AND IRELAND

The problems of an English writer defending a territory are similar in kind but different in degree to those of writers in the non-English cultures of the British Isles...he has to find the words and forms in which the reality of his place and the integrity of his vision may be embodied within a language that works increasingly to spread a uniform placelessness.

Jeremy Hooker (*Poetry of Place*)

I

In the previous chapter, we suggested that the mythical framework which exists at the geographical and social margins be considered from a perspective which views myth as a mode of signification. Unlike the traditional view of myth, which theoretical writings originating from the margins themselves have followed, this post-structuralist perspective, as we shall see later, highlights the problematic nature of the relationship which often exists between many poets at the margins and the modes of signification in which they work. However, as we argued, the emphasis upon a more traditional model of myth does reflect a profound concern in these areas with tradition and continuity, a concern which has given historical debates about myth in Wales and Ireland a particular slant. A concern with continuity, ancestry, culture and identity unites writers working in Wales and Ireland with those of working-class origins in the North of England. Of course, most of what we have to say of working-class poets in the North of England applies to poets of similar origins from other parts of England, Wales, Ireland and Scotland. But

the North of England does have a more problematic relationship to the conventional parameters of cultural power than that
of many other areas. This gives the region a special significance
for this study and a special kind of parity with Wales and Ireland. In the latter regions, as we have already stressed, the
framework in which poets work is highly politicised and in the
North of England it is equally difficult for poets not to see their
ancestry — familial and social — in other than highly politicised terms.

In the North of England there are a number of centres of
poetry such as the North East and West Yorkshire. Hudders-
field, for example, has been described — only half-jokingly —
as Britain's poetry capital. Yet these centres are not the centres
of movements and within each region's work there is considerable diversity. The flowering of poetry in these areas must not
be confused with the emergent rôle of Liverpool as a centre of
poetry in the 1960s; then poetry flourished in, and because of,
its relationship with music. The new flowering of poetry in the
North owes more to the existence of support groups — such as
those established in West Yorkshire in the wake of the miners'
strike in the second half of the 1980s — and creative writing
classes and societies.

Neil Astley, in writing of poetry from the North-East of England, reminds us that concentrating upon local, social or contemporary issues can often result in the production of minor art:
"to narrow one's perspective to that of a 'local writer'; a political
spokesman or a journalist."[1] He argues for a broader sense of
regional consciousness in which regional experience is recognised as one, albeit an important, aspect of the writer's identity
and for poets who, in trying to define the Northern experience,
keep their concerns wide.[2] Astley is, of course, writing about a
region that has been opened up by the presence of an international literary journal, Stand, so that "the North-East's literary
tradition has become not folk-based but international in out-
look." Indeed, as Astley points out, several Northern poets are
also distinguished translators: notably Bunting, Harrison, Elliot
and Adcock.[3]

According to Astley, there are two types of North-East poetry,
underpinned by a concern with regional culture and identity.
One type of writing he rejects as too parochial and narrow.

31

Little of this work "is distinguishable, rhythmically, from prose, and much of it consists of sentimental journalism or jokey auto-biography...."[4] The other type of writing is that in which the "poets are contributing to the mainstream of English poetry" and which must "not be separated from its national context".[5] Unfortunately, Astley fails to define what he means by main-stream, for mainstream is often used to refer to poetry originating in or associated with the London literary establishment.

Two key works by Northern poets, Jeffrey Wainwright's *The Important Man* (1970) and James Longwill's 'Bobby Arnet' (1977), are characterised by an approach to history which is itself indebted, indirectly or directly, consciously or unconsciously, to E.P. Thompson's epoch-making *The Making of the English Working Class*. Wainwright's origins, of course, are in Stoke-on-Trent rather than the North-East, but his work was undoubtedly influenced by literary developments in the North-East. *The Important Man* was itself produced by a North-East publishing house and much of his work was originally published in *Stand*.

Both these poets, like many others from the North-East, approach history — because of their social and familial ancestries — from the perspective of the lower classes and focus on the individual. In doing so, however, they avoid the trap of seeing history as made up of the interventions of famous men and women acting as free agents. Their poetry presents the contributions of individual men and women as one of a number of factors, not least the complex interaction of classes, institutions and modes of production.

That a poet from the North should choose to write political poems around historical themes may seem curious to a reader from outside of the region. After all, poetry reaches such a small, and reasonably élite, audience that there are more effective ways of initiating political change. But to anyone born into the North, of working-class origins, a sense of identity is inevitably bound up with the history and the gradual politicisation of working-class consciousness.

Whereas Seamus Heaney's work, like that of many Celtic, and especially Northern Ireland, poets since the Second World War, opposes the order of poetry to the discontinuity of history, the mainland has seen an increasing tendency for poets to use his-

tory as a way of explaining, and of giving order to, the frag-
mented and chaotic present. History gives what has happened
in the industrial areas a structure and a kind of logic.

II

Jeffrey Wainwright interprets issues of culture and identity
against a broader canvas than that of Tony Harrison who, although born in Leeds, has also been very much associated with
the North-East. As Jeremy Hooker in a short, but sympathetic
essay on Wainwright (both were for a short time colleagues in
the English Department at the University College of Wales,
Aberystwyth) has pointed out:

> Nor is he like Tony Harrison, a poet who writes from a fully
> developed sense of himself, as autobiographical subject, divided
> between the love and pain of his original working-class home and
> the world into which academic and literary success has introduced
> him.[6]

Wainwright tends to focus upon figures from history involved
in periods of crisis. 'The Mad Talk of George III' is told in
George III's voice and underpinned by the fact that non-stop
talk was one of the characteristics of George's illness. The poem
is rooted in the suggestion that the monarch might have been
driven mad by the upheaval of the age in which he ruled. After
all, the period from 1760-1820 saw enormous changes such as
the American Revolution, the French Revolution, the Industrial
Revolution and the ushering in of the whole era of democracy
when ideas of Kingship and authority were in question. George
III is seen by Wainwright as an old figure with a fearful, pessimistic notion of the world. This is balanced by a more romantic
world-view in 'A Hymn to Liberty' which appropriately focuses
upon a child as the image of the unrealised future and of unrealised potential, a theme developed at length in 'Five Winter
Songs'.[7]
In Wainwright's work, the interest in high status, important
figures is opposed to an interest in ordinary people who are
usually victims. It is a perspective rooted in the mythical framework of the North — employing the concept of myth as a mode
of signification — in which Wainwright seeks orientation and

definition. The mill-girl — the titular subject of the first poem of the sequence '1815' — like Heaney's girl in 'Punishment', a poem which we will discuss later, is a victim, although of a different kind and in different circumstances. Wainwright's poem focuses upon the callous perspective of industrial, capitalist society which sees the individual only as an insignificant part of a larger system, so it is appropriate that we never learn the girl's name for, unlike her body in death, she was never allowed to "rise".

The movement of the poem from the individual girl to the collective "apprentices, jiggers, spinners" is rooted in the mythical framework of the North of England. It signifies the system that has no respect for the individual and can bury people together with only the smallest, most economic, space between them. Wainwright's pun, "the graves have not / A foot's width between them", refers to both the measurement of twelve inches and a foot of a human corpse. Such sharp, mordant wit is a major agent of control in Wainwright's poetry, directing the criticism and holding several layers of meaning together. Indeed, many of Wainwright's sharpest puns are macabre in their references to death, highlighting the appalling indifference of industrial society to the sanctity of life and to the individual. The above pun neatly encapsulates the expendability of the working classes and the attitude of the bosses towards their employees. The other puns in the poem reinforce these points. The apprentices, jiggers and spinners fill the graves "straight from work / Common as smoke." The phrase, "straight from work", relates to finishing the working shift, but also refers to the fact there is no retirement as such: workers do not live long enough to enjoy that final break from work! Moreover, there is a strong suggestion again that these people are easily dispensable. "Common as smoke" is deliberately ambiguous. "Common", on one level, suggests the way these people are not given the opportunity to become cultured, to be anything more than "common". "Common" is, of course, an epithet used by the cultured of people they regard as uncultured suggesting, as does Tony Harrison in 'Them and [Uz]', that culture as a part of a larger value system, is rooted in the political system, and is related to the notion of one group having power and control over another. But "common" also reinforces again the expendability of the workers in economic terms: there is an unending supply of labour. It is significant that in using the word "common" in this way, Wainwright links issues of culture with issues of economic power.

As we said in the introduction, readers are drawn to poetry not for political wisdom and insight, but for the experience of the language. Wainwright's poem says little new in suggesting that life for the working class in the nineteenth century was brutish and short. But what could be clichéd is saved by the ingenuity of the wit and the language. Moreover, we all know about the farm workers who took naïve pride in enlisting to fight for their country only to meet sudden and premature death, but once again in the second poem of '1815', the poem is kept on the right side of cliché by Wainwright's wit: "The deep-chested rosy ploughboys / swell out of their uniforms." The word "swell" is, once again, ambiguous meaning "swelling with pride" and also "swelling with death".

The wit and the reliance, as in Harrison's case, upon original and sometimes quite startling ambiguities, is rooted in an eye and ear for language often possessed by those who acquire language and education while moving from one class to another. But the fact that Wainwright's working-class origins underpin the employment of wit, irony and ambiguity in '1815' is evident on another level, too. The wit is actually fuelled by a disgust which comes from looking at society from the bottom-up, as it were, and from seeing events from the point of view of the ordinary person. It is so difficult for a sane person to comprehend the extent of the indifference of the system that wit sometimes becomes a way of dealing with the consequent bewilderment and anger. Indeed, the incredulity produces some of Wainwright's best lines in '1815', for example: "Waterloo is all the rage." Here the enthusiasm for Waterloo is encapsulated along with the poet's disgust in the single word "rage" which can also mean anger. Wainwright's contempt for those in authority is reinforced by the way that rage means not just 'enthusiasm for', but an enthusiasm that does not last. The contempt produces other good puns, too: "No flies on Wellington. / His spruce wit sits straight / In the saddle jogging by." Wainwright keeps the stench and the decay of death to the fore through the use of a colloquial expression, while at the same time suggesting the extent to which Wellington is removed from the slaughter. Also encapsulated here is the smug stance of Wellington himself to whom the fallen cavalry are no more than turtles.

III

The highly politicised awareness of history in the North East of England underpins also James Longwill's 'Bobby Arnet (1790-1869)' from *A Man's Jacket* (1977). The poem is a pared rather curt narrative of Bobby's life. Obviously, many years are covered in relatively few lines. But the kind of political tub thumping to which accounts of life from the underdog's point of view are prone is avoided. The style is appropriate in so far as it conveys Bobby's stoicism and, from the age of eighteen when he is pressed into the King's shilling, the minimal control he has over his life. In this sense 'pressed' is not only the right adverb, historically, to describe Bobby's enlistment, but is germane with the way in which he is, as through most of his life, the victim of those with power.

Longwill makes political comment in subtle ways. The statement that Bobby fought in Spain and at Waterloo is juxtaposed with the way in which, on his discharge, he has to walk back north and there find his family has been evicted: "land sold / mortgaged to our neighbours / who bought us out." The details that are selected are representative images of the hardships that Bobby has to endure generally while the house he lived in as a boy becomes symbolic of the ancestral line which is now irretrievably broken. The sudden transition from "Their" to "We" in 'The house' section —

> Their children play
> there now. We made
> its small, red bricks

— signifies the way in which the emergent social mobility is axiomatic with the destruction of deep, ancestral roots in a particular locality. The poem traces Bobby Arnet's developing political awareness. The sections entitled 'The house' and 'Their farm' are separated by a section which looks back to 1802, a year in which he watched "our kid" die of cholera. The juxtaposition belies the grim acceptance of his fate which characterised the first section of the poem and demonstrates his new, emergent "political" consciousness which is also that of his class and which shapes and determines the second half of the poem.

The events of 1802, the floods, the failed harvest, and the destruction of the cattle, contrasts with the prosperity of their farm in 1836 and the slaughter-house full of their beef. The condition of the farm — with "scalded and / salt-scrubbed" dairy and tools with "wooden handles / grained and shining" — stands in contradistinction to the byre of the second section. Most important of all we have the contrast between their children playing and the death of "our kid". While, as the building of the house in the second section of the poem suggests, his family achieved what it had only by toil and effort, they seem to have landed on their feet more easily:

> And now Middlesbrough
> fills with Irish
> they go over to dairy.

The "political" awakening is evinced, and reinforced, by the repetition of "I see": "I see the beasts..."; "I see the dairy's...".

Bobby Arnet's life corresponded with a period of unprecedented social change with which, in the section 'Greatham Creek', he tries to come to terms. The whole section is underpinned by the kind of inner strength which has sustained Bobby through events of the earlier sections of the poem:

> I catch fish there.
> They move like smoke
> under water.
>
> Other days
> I collect driftwood.
> Go to the woods
>
> to kill vermin.
> For six crows
> I get three parish pennies.

The economy of the writing — appropriate because a man like Bobby would have been unable to articulate his experiences in the same way as an educated poet — conveys, without attributing too many literary skills to Bobby, the way in which his sense of his own identity becomes the core of his resistance.

IV

Those writers whom Astley has labelled narrow and parochial have employed description as if it were a mirror image of reality. But the poets who, in opening up the Northern literary scene, have contributed also to the diversity and excellence of British poetry are aware that both "reality" and the depiction of "reality" are shaped by socio-economic forces. The working-class milieu in which they have their origins is not presented nostalgically as an idealised past. Instead, there is a dialectic between themselves and their origins similar to that which we will highlight later in the work of Welsh women poets and which shapes their depiction of community. In both cases, it finds expression in an original and sometimes abrasive use of language.

Many of the poems of George Charlton, for example, are rooted in tensions (rather than conflicts) or in momentarily achieved release from them. For example, the temporary release enjoyed by working-class men in 'Hunting the Hare' can only be fully appreciated by one coming from those origins. It is encapsulated in the image of the track: the orbit itself — "Floodlit as the bright side of the moon " — signifies the self-contained satisfaction of the greyhound race meeting. The description of the hare as "electric" is both literal and figurative. The track is compared to the bright side of the moon and the "hounds *uncoil* from traps" (my italics). The latter echoes also how the men themselves have escaped from "cluttered living rooms" and "belly-aching, boss-eyed wives". Of course, all this is sexist. The men do not think that their wives need release, believing "free gifts" will make up for everything. But the poem is rooted in a working-class culture which prioritises male camaraderie. The main tension within the poem is between the sense of fulfilment and expansion that is achieved — "the full moon's face / Has an image of the hare in it" — and the reality of working-class life which exists only on the edges of this poem as it does on the edges of the race track. The whole thing is illusory as the inflated language highlights: "the aristocrats of Odds"; "the Eldorado of their dreams"; "Chancellors bearing free gifts...".

'Friday Evenings' is similarly organised around a series of binary opposites. Friday evening as a special night in working-class culture has much to do with dream and illusion and, as in 'Hunting the Hare', this is suggested by the inflated language: the men are "clean as water babies"; they are the "heroes of the commonplace". Friday evening, the day on which they are paid, is traditionally a night of drinking, camaraderie and courtship in working-class culture. As in 'Hunting the Hare', the working-life has been pushed out to the edges of the evening and to the edges of the poem, suggested in the image of the star sparkling as if it had been "struck like a welding arc" and the way in which the men have not only had to wash, but scrub to make themselves clean. But reality is there waiting to intrude in the image of the dull light, the varnished pub, the congested ash trays, and the last bus home.

Although these poems are rooted in Northern England, they deal with issues of culture and identity which transcend a particular region. But once again the regional origins give a quality to the writings which distinquishes them from work associated with the London literary establishment. This quality is not just what Astley sees as abrasiveness, but rather a hard-nosed matter-of-factness, evident in the way many — though of course not all — of Charlton's poems come to uncompromising conclusions. 'Sea Coal' concludes with "Bleached tales to the hard-up and out of work, / Rumouring of desolation riding the slack." 'Retired Men' ends on an image of how "Green clotted seawood drifts into the shore. / Their wages stopped some time ago."

Original images are tightly controlled and are hardly ever allowed elaborate development. For example, from 'Night Shift Workers', we have the image of the man living "Inside-out like socks pulled on in darkness." In 'Sea Coal' coal pickers:

Bent-backed on the water fringe balance
Sacks on the cross-bars of clapped out bikes,
Stretch their spines and look out, gazing —

Of course, we find this controlled originality in other works, but in North East writing it is part of a cluster of features that when taken together appear to point to something characteristic of the

North of England. There is also, for example, a controlled sensuality that emerges in poems concerned with relationships; a sensuality that informs startlingly vivid images. In 'The Kiss', one of the 'Postcard Poems': "His tongue along the smooth edge of her teeth / Her mouth warm as an oven, cool as peach". In 'Jugged Hare on Sunday', another 'Postcard Poem': "Your absence, — that warm indifference / Absorbent like the softest tissue paper."

This controlled, abrasive originality is not unrelated to the highly politicised approach to history which we find in some Northern poets. It is indeed "political" in the sense that it is part of the attempt to resist the larger hegemonic forces that would deny their cultural origins; part of the attempt to find a language that will enable them to express their own, resistant sense of identity.·

V

The existence of a sympathetic publishing house — Poetry Wales Press (now known as Seren Books) — committed to publishing Welsh, English-language authors, and its key periodical *Poetry Wales*, have inspired the development of writing in Wales in a similar way to that in which the presses of the North East and the literary periodical, *Stand*, have opened up that area. The international dimension of *Stand*, too, is to be found in a slightly different format in Wales in the periodical, *Planet*. The poet, Nigel Jenkins, has confessed that: "I was reading *Planet*... I felt very sympathetic to its determined idea of Wales in the centre of the world, rather than Oxford or Cambridge or London, and to the openness to other parts of the world, and especially minority cultures."[8] In June 1988, a new periodical, *The New Welsh Review*, was established with a commitment to "publishing excellent English language writing from all parts of the world."

As in the North East, the concern with culture and identity in the best contemporary poetry from Wales is neither narrow nor parochial. This is especially true of those poets writing in the English language from the urban areas. Wales, of course, enters their work explicitly and implicitly through history, through a sense of place and through the choice of thematic concerns. But, as we suggested earlier, it is not highlighted in the same way as it is in the work of R.S. Thomas and Raymond Garlick. Robert Minhinnick has said: "My neighbours are real people with individual identities before they are instruments used to depict what Welsh life is like in the twentieth century. 'Smith's Garage' might be said to be political, in the sense that you could see the description of a derelict industrial site as a metaphor for the present state of Wales. But that would be too easy."[9]

Two of the poles of Robert Minhinnick's imagination are the sea (and the beach) and the industrial heritage of South Wales. At first, they may seem to be very different areas of interest. But they are brought together in a profound concern with time, erosion, and resistance, and an interest in the ordinary life of the region. These themes are axiomatic with the particular historical perspective we discussed earlier and which we find in many of the poets from the urban, industrial areas of Wales — Mike Jenkins, for example — as well as those of the North of England — Harrison, Wainwright, Charlton, for example. As in their work, Minhinnick's "world might be described as the underside of late, decayed capitalist society. It is a kind of underworld, not of subhumanity, but of people exploited and pushed aside, of the defeated — Minhinnick has a Gissing-like sympathy with them — and of crafty or precarious survivors, poachers, mechanics, the unemployed."[10]

The titular poem of *The Dinosaur Park* epitomises Minhinnick's response to the passing of the age of heavy industry in South Wales and to the legacy left within the landscape and the people. At one point in the poem, a metaphor suddenly makes the covert imaginative connection between the dinosaur and heavy industry explicit:

> And then the other trespassers,
> Bolted on to sandy plinths,
> Moored in the wrong time.
> Out of the fantastic past they loom,
> Great engines seized, the inert
> Mechanics of some botched experiment.

The language here — "Bolted", "Moored", "Great engines" and "inert / Mechanics" — suggests the great age of Welsh industry, remnants of which now "loom" out of "the fantastic past" like the statues of the reptiles.

As Jeremy Hooker reminds us: "Poets who are borderers between a world of mental and verbal skills and a world of manual labour on which they are practically and imaginatively
dependent, share a common effort to remember and do justice
to the latter."[11] But *The Dinosaur Park* also displays Minhinnick's
tendency to search the vast expanse of time for a deeper sense
of shared experience at different points on the continuum of
what he calls, 'Natural History':

> These postures struck of combat,
> Rage, the slow acknowledging of pain.
> And strange to think such creatures shared
> The common factors of our lives,
> Hurt and hunger, fear of death,
> The gradual discovery of betrayal.

As well as poems of worked-out places and monuments to the
industrial past, there are poems concerned with relics of ordinary life washed up or half buried along shore lines which
become images of resistance against the larger forces of time
and decay. In 'The Coast': "a shattered bottle reassures that our
claim / Was made." And throughout *The Dinosaur Park*, Minhinnick is interested in the way in which human life has been
tied up with these objects:

> History is not this gear of bronze,
> Its patina teal-green;
> Rather, it is how it was used,
> The association of metal and mind.

Jeremy Hooker has drawn attention to how Minhinnick's
"feeling for the social and working life of places such as garages
and pubs and the kitchen and garden side of country estates
suggests a family history underpinning his poetic craft."[12] In
many ways, this "feeling" is one of the chief characteristics of
Minhinnick's work as Hooker suggests. But there is another
dimension which needs stressing: the sense of detachment. In
some respects 'Grandfather in the Garden' is similar to Heaney's 'Digging', a poem which we will come to later. Like Heaney, Minhinnick admires his forefather's skill and feels he has
inherited much from him: "He taught patience in slow lessons /
And one man's dedication to a craft." But, like Heaney, he him-

self does not share his grandfather's manual dexterity: "Digging was always my worst work."

Unlike in Heaney's work, entropy, decay and the way in which toil can wear an individual down are all emphasised:

> Late evenings I'd be sent
> To call him in, a dark and elemental
> Shape by then, the ruins of a young man's face
> Still visible behind the years, the toil. [53]

The sense of dislocation which Minhinnick feels when confronting this manual life is the linchpin of 'The Tack Room':

> His room describes another way
> Of life, a different point of view.
> Uncalloused hands find only
> Hostility in its warped boards

The prefix 'un' reinforces the poet's sense of being, and having been, separated from the family norm. It is underlined further by the cumulative effect of "another", "different" and "only / Hostility". Whatever feeling there is in this poem towards what the tack room represents is held in check in favour of an overwhelming sense of detachment. Nearly everything the poet sees distances him: "These nails, cold hundreds, in regiments"; "the oiled immaculate body / Of the vice"; and the "measured out" drills.

Moreover, as in the work of George Charlton and other poets of the North East, there is friction between the poet and his environment which undercuts any nostalgia for a working-class past. Indeed, the latter is overtly resisted, as is clear from 'Big Pit, Blaenafon': [54]

> Under the rock a museum of work
> And death; their illusions of dignity.
> We see what we should never have believed.

Like the North-East poets, the articulate poet of *The Dinosaur Park* is aware of the inarticulate around him: "When you are born dumb / There are only gestures to make." In 'The Saltings', a strong sense of the life and the human potential which have been thwarted merges through the references to "the women [as] grizzled wands", sparse grass and the child pressed under its mother's heart like a fossil. Minhinnick is sympathetic to the underdog, but, unlike some of the North East poets, seems frightened of some of the ways in which the inarticulate classes express their defiance. Symbols of these acts of defiance recur in the work with hints of menace. In 'At "The Knights" ' there are symbols of swastikas and empty cider cans buckled in half, all of which stand in opposition to the word "L.O.V.E." on the youth's knuckles.

VI

This politicised view of history which is very much part of the Northern poet's ancestry and the mythical framework in which he or she tries to find orientation and definition unites Northern, Welsh and Irish poetry. From the whirlpool of Northern Ireland cultures, a number of important poets have emerged since the late 1960s with as sharp an edge to their voices: of these, apart from Seamus Heaney, Derek Mahon, Michael Longley, Paul Muldoon and Tom Paulin are the most notable. Their work is varied and each develops a quite distinctive range of poetic possibilities. So much so that to generalise about the development of modern poetry in contemporary Northern Ireland is to risk grave distortions. But in a comparison of their response to history with that which we find in the work of Welsh, English-language poets and Northern England poets, some patterns do emerge. It is impossible not to see how Northern Irish poetry "has been unable to entirely evade a confrontation with Irish history although it finds various strategies of deflection and even of escape in order to preserve some vestige of independence from it".[13] In this respect alone we can see how Seamus Heaney fits into this larger literary context, but there are other recurring aspects of Northern Ireland poetry with which Heaney's work has affinities: the isolation of the artistic sensibility and the desire to give voice to what is unspoken, to the voiceless, even the forgotten.[14]

Northern Ireland poetry demonstrates how history and politics are sometimes desperately intertwined. In this respect, Mahon's universally acclaimed 'A Disused Shed' really is a pivotal poem. The mushrooms, in the penultimate verse, become a key signifier. They have endured: "A half century, without visitors, in the dark —". The line is carefully structured to end on the word 'dark' so as to anticipate the light that does come. And it comes as a shock, for which the "cracking lock" and "creak of hinges" hardly prepare us: "At the flash-bulb firing squad we wake them with / Shows there is life yet in their feverish forms." As throughout Mahon's work, we are reminded of the violence of Northern Ireland. While there is no liberation for the "powdery prisoners", there is an emergent faith in the power of poetry to transform and redeem: "Grown beyond nature now, soft food for worms, / They lift frail heads in gravity and good faith."

Edna Longley suggests that Mahon's symbol of the mushrooms is actually borrowed by Muldoon in 'Gathering Mushrooms' from *Quoof* (1983).[15] Critics often contrast Muldoon with Paulin rather than with Mahon: the one concerned with "a poetry of denial", the other with "commitment".[16] Such a view is fairer to Muldoon than Paulin, for Edna Longley is near the mark when she maintains: "Muldoon's methods give the lie to the notion that language can operate politically in Irish poetry only by declaring firm allegiances."[17] The kind of political motive we have in Muldoon's work is that "of escaped prisoner-of-war, secret agent, double agent, saboteur." Longley demonstrates this by pointing out how 'The More a Man Has the More a Man Wants', which concludes *Quoof*, "disconcerts on a larger scale as it juggles with tenses and moods, history, literary history, place and name, an anarchic version of sonnet-form, and a cosmopolitan vocabulary."[18]

In all of this, we have the distinctively un-English way of using English that we find in the work of many Welsh, English-language and Northern England poets. We also have the desire, evident in many contemporary poets from these regions, but never so consciously and deliberately expressed as in Muldoon's case, "to blow the whistle on the conspiracy between myth and cliché".[19] The Welsh, the Northern Irish and the Northern English poets are often all too well aware of "the booby" traps in phrases, frequently concerning themselves with, to adapt Longley, "how poetry remakes language, wears it new, acts as a midwife to a future not *predicated* on the past"[20] (my italics). This does not make them indifferent to, ignorant of or hopelessly exclusive of the past, but aware of the need to "meet or expand rigid understandings of history".[21] The problematic and highly politicised mythical framework in which Northern Ireland, North of England and Welsh poets work and seek the orientation and definition of which we have already spoken impels a recurring concern in their work with the rôle of the poet.

Like Heaney, Muldoon is frequently concerned with justifying his rôle as a poet. In 'Lunch with Pancho Villa' from *Mules* (1977) Muldoon is criticised by the men-of-action against whom Heaney tried to define, and defend, his own rôle as a poet:

> 'Look, son. Just look around you.
> People are getting themselves killed
> Left, right and centre
> While you do what? Write rondeaux?
> There's more to living in this country
> Than stars and horses, pigs and trees,
> Not that you'd guess it from your poems'.

The word, "son", is a familiar colloquialism, but it also implicates the poet as a child of Ireland. Yet Muldoon sees a value in "rambling on" about "pigs and trees, and stars and horses", articulating the ordinary life of Northern Ireland. This is not to say that he does not feel involved in the violence within Ulster. Throughout his work — in, for example, 'Field Hospital' and 'The Bearded Woman, by Ribera' — there is the image of the stranger (the image of the stranger and images of alienation recur in contemporary Irish poetry) somewhat removed yet implicated in what is going on. In many ways, this epitomises the approach throughout Muldoon's poetry for he frequently juxtaposes different viewpoints without committing himself to any particular one. It also accords with the way in which the emblematic, at times enigmatic, nature of his work suggests that "truth" is something which cannot be easily discovered or too simply trusted.

In this respect, Muldoon is a very different poet from Paulin. If Edna Longley is near the mark in her discussion of Muldoon, she is off target in her view of Paulin whom she often introduces derogatorily in comparison with him.[22] There is a great deal in Paulin's poetry that Longley avoids: ironic humour, the poignant solitariness, the painful or sardonic alienation of the émigré. Muldoon "wants a freedom for poetry".[23] Longley can understand and admire that, but Paulin is not her kind of poet. He insists, as Seamus Deane says, that "poetry should be grounded in a political reality and contribute to an enriched sense of community".[24] But he also seeks "liberation from factional politics".[25] He presents, as Terry Eagleton has said, "a rural political discourse to the 'book of the tribe', the lurid biblical rhetoric of loyalism...".

Very few, hardly any, of the poets we have mentioned so far stand in an easy relationship with their native ground. At times Paulin welcomes release:

> The release of putting off
> who and where we've come from
> then meeting in this room
> with no clothes on —
> to believe in nothing,
> to be nothing.

But there is also the "reality" of an empty motorway and a transit van packed with gauze sacks; an alienation reinforced by images of solitariness and ground mist. Political realities entwined with history which Paulin cannot gainsay push him further into this sense of alienation as is suggested in 'An Ulster Unionist Walks the Streets of London':

> I waited outside the gate-lodge,
> waited like a dog
> in my own province
> till a policeman brought me
> a signed paper.
> Was I meant to beg
> and be grateful?

A similar sense of isolation informs 'Fivemiletown': "I smoked a cigarette / while an olive armoured car / nosed down the hill —." Here Paulin seems to be recalling the famous Strand advertisement featuring a gaberdined stranger who is seen alone and smoking a cigarette. The Strand advertisement campaign was unsuccessful because it failed to understand that the public perceived smoking as a social not a solitary activity. But, thereafter, the stranger in the gaberdine became a symbol of alienation, of solitariness. Here that image is recreated and placed in a new context which underscores it. The sense of alienation is intensified by the surveillance of the armoured car which does not simply move past, but is said to have "nosed", a word which highlights the intrusion which it is impossible not to feel in such a circumstance. Paulin's work represents a poetry which is politicised without being "sentimental or emotional" in "a way that is dangerous to oneself and others".

The recommendations that "to trust anyone or to admit any hope of a better world is criminally foolish" and that poets should "work without hope" which Longley argues are "detrumescent" for those "who crave poetry in their politics and politics in their poetry" are themselves part of an extreme political strategy, rooted in particular circumstances, and needing to be handled cautiously out of its context.[27] What we see in many contemporary poets — even in the work of Muldoon and Paulin themselves — is not often as simple as the adoption of one position in preference to another, but the jostling of different stances and strategies in tension. The poets in this study take on the "burden of culture, the interrogation of the links that connect us to, or in breaking, disconnect us from the idea of a social community".[28]

In these introductory chapters, we have suggested that the work of poets writing from positions outside the conventional parameters of cultural power is best approached through the mythical framework in which they seek orientation and definition. We have also suggested that this approach is dependent upon a post-structuralist concept of myth as a mode of signification rather than the traditional view of myth which some theoretical writings originating from the social and geographical margins have tended to stress. While this framework helps us to understand the preoccupations with ancestry, culture and identity which unite much of the work written at the margins, it often highlights the way in which many of these poets are struggling against aspects of this mythical framework in order to achieve what it undercuts or denies. This, together with a highly politicised concern with history and with the processes of hegemony, impels also a self-conscious concern with the rôle of the poet.

In Part Two, we shall consider the work of the poets writing from different positions outside the social and economic centre, united by their concern with culture and identity, within the frameworks within which they seek orientation and definition.

PART TWO

SIX CONTEMPORARY POETS

CHAPTER THREE

FROM THE LAND OF THE UNSPOKEN: MAPPING HEANEY'S COURSE

Our poesy is as a gum which oozes
From whence 'tis nourished.
        Shakespeare (*Timon of Athens*)

I

As Elmer Andrews has summarised: "It is only when we attend to the details of Heaney's recreation of the rural world that we find implications of a larger social and moral order, an inheritance for which the poet feels incapacitated by his own sensibility. There is a notion of discontinuity, a feeling of loss, a sense of guilt, an apprehension of violence as well as of beauty and mystery, lying deep in things."[1] For these reasons, and because Heaney — born and brought up in Northern Ireland — insists he is an Irish and not a British poet, he must have a central place in any discussion of issues of culture, ancestry and identity in contemporary poetry. There is a preoccupation with cultural processes in his work which deserves as much attention as some of the other political aspects of his poetry.

The increasing emphasis given to the political concerns of the later work (before *The Haw Lantern*) has led to the earlier poetry being virtually dismissed as merely a pastoral phase. This chapter reviews the critical tradition concerning Heaney's work focusing upon the way in which some of the key issues of the early work — cultural processes, hegemony and legitimation — have been underemphasised. This study highlights Heaney's interest in the dynamic between ancestry, culture and personal fulfilment, his longstanding interest in an imaginative holism as a counterpoint to historical determinism, and the way in which many of the cultural issues he raises are clearly embodied in the male-female opposition within his work.

The way in which Heaney's rural, working-class background was a formative influence upon his consciousness is evident from 'Alphabets' in *The Haw Lantern* (1987) where he remembers having learned his letters from his father. The poem begins with an early, pre-school memory of his father casting an image with his hands of a rabbit on to a wall which suggests that the process of imaging, so important to Heaney as a poet, was actually inherited, consciously or unconsciously, from his father. His father taught him not only to think in images, but passed on a rural culture and sensibility — as the process by which Heaney learned to read and write reveals: *Y* is a forked stick; *2* is a swan, *A* is two rafters with a cross-tie; "English" is marked correct with "a little leaning hoe".

Heaney's respect for his skilled, rural forefathers is embodied in many of the early poems. In 'Digging' in *Death of a Naturalist* he declares with wonder: "By God, the old man could handle a spade / Just like his old man." The pride which his grandfather had in cutting more turf in a day than any other man on Toner's bog is reborn in the respect and pride which his grandson still has for that achievement. And, equally important, the poet inherits his forefathers' sensuous awareness of nature. Hence, Heaney's early verse, as many critics have pointed out, is rich with attention to detail and the luscious rendering of sound. This inheritance as a cultural as well as a familial legacy pervades the first part of *Death of a Naturalist*.

Of course, these poems were written in hindsight, the poet separated from the initial experiences by age and education. Clotted with sound and colour, they often suggest too strongly someone reclaiming a sensibility of which he has become bereft. But the way in which 'Death of a Naturalist' stresses the contrast between the poet-as-young-boy's awareness, the intensity of which the poetry tries to recreate, and the school teacher's interpretation of the boy's experience is pertinent to our argument:

Miss Walls would tell us how
The daddy frog was called a bullfrog
And how he croaked and how the mammy frog
Laid hundreds of little eggs and this was
Frogspawn.

The latter is patronising and she makes no attempt to help the boy articulate his experience of nature. Her lesson, dispelling the miraculous by its deliberate, mental profligacy, has to be seen within the context of the title of the poem: *'Death* of a Naturalist' (my italics). Her name is appropriately "Miss Walls" for she creates only barriers and erects walls against development.

Miss Walls and this early disabusing experience of education have broader connotations. The depredations of the education system to which Heaney was introduced were essentially English, and the more bitterly resented for that. With the realisation that schooling was but a weapon in the armoury of colonialisation, the process of politicisation in Heaney's poetry began, as the imagery of the last part of the poem, 'Death of a Naturalist', with references to grenades, threats, and vengeance suggests.

While, on one level, 'Death of a Naturalist', like many of the early poems, is about knowledge and about a child growing out of innocence, its focus upon education severing connections with a native, inherited sensibility is embedded in an emergent political critique of cultural processes. This critique dominates much of the later work, not least the poem 'Alphabets', with which we opened this discussion. Because Heaney learns that there is a right and a wrong way to hold a pen, because his work is marked correct or incorrect and because A is a letter some pronounce *"ah"* and others *"ay"* the poem adumbrates how a child is inducted unwittingly into the hierarchy of culture: a bold assertion, but borne out by the way the "coloured O" anticipates the "wooden O" of Shakespeare's Globe Theatre later in the poem.

We shall see later how education and the acquisition of formal, correct English became one of the bones of contention between Tony Harrison and his father. In a similar sense, education separated Heaney from his mother. Like Harrison, he feels guilty about this, recalling in the sequence of poems devoted to his mother's death how at home he lapsed into dialect so that he and his mother did not fall out with each other. The poems, like many of the poems in *The Haw Lantern*, are about guilt, conflict, disorientation and betrayal. Like Harrison, Heaney cannot forsake his talents and education. He feels he is betraying his education and what he has learned by relapsing "into the wrong / Grammar which kept us allied and at bay." His mother affects inadequacy:

> as if she might betray
> The hampered and inadequate by too
> Well-adjusted a vocabulary.

The poetry is rooted, though, not just in the experiences of disorientation and alienation, but the socio-political, post-colonial factors which have brought them about and which in the development of Heaney's work were to receive greater emphasis.

As an Irish writer working in the English language, Heaney recognises — is forced to recognise — that the Irish language belongs to the past. In 'The Backwood Look' in *Wintering Out*, the snipe flees its native ground as language has done. At the end of the poem, we find both snipe and language only among "gleanings and leavings / in the combs / of a field worker's archive." The loss of language in Ireland, as in Wales, is part of a larger process of dispossession and despoliation. In 'Traditions' the way "our guttural muse / was bulled long ago / by the alliterative tradition" is acknowledged and accepted, but what is resented is the way that the Ulster dialect has been refashioned and the way in which the English have denigrated language and Irish cultural traditions. The recreations of the skills of Heaney's forefathers in poems such as 'Digging', then, are more than reconstructions of familial traditions. They are recreations of ancestral pride and self-respect in the face of the lingering effects of colonialisation. Critical discussions of many of the early poems have tended to ignore this context and have treated the reconstructions as if they were autonomous.

'Follower' and 'Digging', both in *Death of a Naturalist*, are rediscoveries of his father and grandfather and also of their crafts underpinned by an emergent, politicised view of culture. We are asked, as readers, to view these skills from a particular, sympathetic perspective. Implicit assumptions have been made about us as readers as regards our knowledge of, and our usually held attitudes towards, these crafts. Thus, in 'Follower', the second word of the first line of the second verse has a strategic emphasis:

> An expert.
> He would set the wing
> And fit the bright steel-pointed sock.
> The sod rolled over without breaking.

It draws our attention not just to his father's proficiency, but to what such proficiency involves:

> His eye
> Narrowed and angled at the ground,
> Mapping the furrow exactly.

The word "exactly", placed pertinently at the end of a line, reinforces the accuracy which he did not need any tools or equipment to achieve while "mapping" suggests the enormity of skill required. As in 'Digging', the poet is humbled by comparison: "I stumbled in his hob-nailed wake...."

Heaney's adroit ancestors and the craftsmen and labourers of the older, rural Ireland in which his origins lie are characterised, however, not only by their skill, by their commitment to their craft and by their physical stamina, but by the way in which they go about their work in a silence which the poet because of his education and art does not share. The attention given to the latter again reflects Heaney's increasingly politicised awareness of cultural processes.

Morrison has demonstrated how "what links the various traders, labourers and craftsmen who fill his first two books is that, unlike him [Heaney], they are lacking in speech." The water-diviner, the Lough Neagh fishermen, the fieldworkers in 'The Wife's Tale' and the thatcher all work silently.[2] In what Morrison calls this "culture of clamped silence", others manage only "a half-utterance from the back of the throat". Hence, as Morrison points out, in the first book "curt" is the most popular adjective and "curtly" the most popular adverb; noise becomes a threat, and the most common sounds are yelps, grunts, gulps, snores, whoops, and coughs.[3]

The way in which *Death of a Naturalist* and *Door into the Dark* seem to be "valuing silence above speech, of defending the shy and awkward against the confident and accomplished, of feeling language to be a kind of betrayal"[4] is ostensibly paradoxical for a poet who owes his living to words. Yet it makes sense in terms of the working-class, Irish, rural community from which Heaney came. As Morrison maintains, this background is not just working-class (as in Harrison's case), it is Northern Irish and Catholic: "He grew up in a culture of the 'siege mentality', where Catholics were always suspected (often justifiably) of harbouring IRA arms and activists...".[5] The argument is developed by Eileen Cahill: "In *Wintering Out* quotation, the recitation of place names, and a sense of stammering enact verbally the Northern Catholic's oppression into silence, but Heaney's linguistic interest makes that silence politically vocal."[6] Heaney's strong, silent craftspeople acted as "models for the poet: as he celebrates them, so they in turn guide and sanction his craft."[7] These craftspeople are also important to Heaney, for the same reasons as Raymond Williams' ancestors in the 'Border Country' between Wales and England were important to him. Inarticulate, or at best only partially articulate, they possessed a depth of feeling with which they were able to resist the hegemony that threatened to destroy the older, rural culture in which Heaney's roots were planted. The parallels between Heaney's work and *Irish Folk Ways*, to which Morrison has drawn attention, suggest that the latter, which warned how "knowledge of ways of life that have altered little for centuries is passing away", was a key influence upon the poet.[8]

The increasing importance Heaney came to place upon this "structure of feeling", to employ Raymond Williams' famous phrase, as a defence against hegemony was responsible for his interest shifting from the traditional skills themselves to the world-view of those who possessed them. 'Thatcher', in *Door into the Dark*, for example, begins: "Bespoke for weeks, he turned up some morning / Unexpectedly...." Here Heaney has taken great care to encapsulate the dissembling insouciance of old, rural Ireland. The seeming carefreeness is maintained in the way in which his bicycle is "slung / With a light ladder..." and the way in which he spends "the morning warming up". But the nonchalance of the first few lines of the poem is undermined by the strategic way in which the man settles to work. The accumulation of verbs — "eyed", "poked", "flicked", "twisted", "fixed", "snipped", "sharpened" — conveys the way in which the thatcher displays the same silent commitment, dynamism, precision, skill, and physical stamina as Heaney's father while ploughing and his grandfather while digging.

The seeming nonchalance, camouflaging the traditional skills, is rooted in a balanced attitude to life enjoyed by those immersed in rural ways and it is with this "sense of life" in the face of larger, hegemonic forces that Heaney is really concerned. How important this became for Heaney personally as a poet is evinced, especially, in 'The Forge'. The blacksmith's traditional craft in 'The Forge' is a surrogate of artistic endeavour. The "unpredictable fantail of sparks" suggests the unpredictable directions in which the poet's writing might develop, the darkness of the forge suggests the unconscious, maybe even the past, while the hiss of the hot shoe in water suggests, perhaps, the reception of his work! The ends of the anvil itself, one square and the other horned like a unicorn, actually signify the two poles of Heaney's imagination: the realistic and the mythical. The blacksmith, like the poet, practises a craft which has its own articulation, contrasted with "outside" where old axles and iron hoops lie rusting and with the blacksmith's memory of "a clatter / Of hoofs where traffic is flashing in rows." There is an integrity in his artistry which is not to be found in, and is not appreciated by, the brash world of contemporary Northern Ireland.

The blacksmith's "grunt" which has been cited by Morrison as an example of the ancestry of silence from which Heaney came, is only a partial response to the way things have changed. More important is the way in which he returns to the anvil, as the poet to his verse, "with a slam and flick / To beat real iron out, to work the bellows." As in the description of the thatcher, the short, sharp verbs encapsulate the skilled work through which the blacksmith (like the poet) really communicates: "expends himself in shape and music".

In the early poems then, traditional lifestyles and crafts are literally centralised by the poet against a threatening, destructive hegemony. The blacksmith's anvil is in the centre of the forge: "set there immoveable". The salmon fisher, likewise, stands in the centre of the stream with the river "cramming" under him. In 'The Plantation', any point is a centre. The field-workers in 'The Wife's Tale' lie in a "ring of their own crusts and dregs". The pride such people have in their work is the crux of their resistance against social movements that would deny and/ or erode what they have to offer. At the end of 'The Forge', the epithet "real iron" emphasises the value of the black-smith's work, the value of the thatcher's work is similarly stressed by the way in which he is said to have a "Midas touch", while the farmer in 'The Wife's Tale' is as "proud as if he were the land itself". Such pride and sense of inner satisfaction are axiomatic with being in touch with an older holism. Hence, at the end of 'The Wife's Tale' the fieldworkers "still kept their ease / Spread out, unbuttoned, grateful, under the trees." What we have is a community and a way of life informed by natural rhythms which are also distinctive, cultural legacies.

Heaney's concern that the reader, as much as himself, discovers and revalues his native, rural Ireland is part of an overall attempt to reclaim his national past. Like the Welsh, English-language poet, Gillian Clarke, who, as we shall see, in 'Letter from a Far Country', draws attention to the historical processes which have defined and legitimated the rôles and representations of women in Welsh culture, Heaney explores and exposes the cultural processes which have legitimated particular versions of the past. For both Heaney and Clarke, this historically-determined framework of constructed meanings in which they seek orientation and definition is crucial.

As Morrison has pointed out, there were two important influences upon Heaney's attitude towards the past. Firstly, that of the 'Belfast Group' to which Heaney belonged which was part of "a larger movement among Northern Irish intellectuals in the 1960s towards the rehabilitation of Ulster's cultural traditions". Secondly, that of the rural anthropology undertaken by E. Estyn Evans in *Irish Folk Ways* (1957). The latter has descriptions of thatching, churning, cattle-dealing, ploughing and forging which form the basis of poems in *Death of a Naturalist* and

Door into the Dark.[9] But Morrison's account stresses "the past" in which Heaney became increasingly interested as a result of these influences rather than the greater awareness of the concepts of hegemony, legitimation, and cultural stratification which they also gave him.

Heaney's developing interest in cultural and historical processes often impels the linguistic inventiveness of *Death of a Naturalist*. While the work in 'Digging' and 'Follower' gave respect and dignity to his forefathers and was an integral part of their individuality and identity, the labouring in 'At a Potato Digging' takes both away. Hence, the workers are seen as a "swarm"; "like crows attacking crow-black fields"; like an army in the way some of them break "ranks"; and like supplicants at prayer. The confusion of metaphors is appropriate to the higgledy-piggledy nature of the work itself, conducted in the wake of a mechanical digger that "wrecks" and "spins".

The central focus of the poem is upon the potato famine as a fact of Irish history which still conditions present day attitudes. The thesis is reinforced by the way in which the structure of the poem itself dovetails the past and the present and by the way in which key words and images from one section are recalled in another: in section one, the line of workers is "higgledy", but, in section three, dealing with the famine itself, the skeletons are "higgledy"; the good potatoes of section two are "live skulls, blind-eyed", but, in section three, the starving have "live skulls, blind-eyed"; and in the last section, the dead from the famine are recalled when the workers flop "dead-beat". Heaney is not concerned with the verisimilitude of the famine for its own sake. The vivacity of the description demonstrates the power of this piece of history for those alive today.

II

'At a Potato Digging' has not only a broader historical perspective than many of the early poems, but a more politicised one. The world-view is closer to that which we described in Part One of this study, informing a more tempered, though not necessarily less effective or less exciting, language. In fact, Heaney's interest in reclaiming his past and the weight of accumulated, historical experience handed down to him through various cultural processes seems to have prompted the movement away from his early, self-conscious style with its over-reliance upon alliteration and onomatopoeia, pilloried by Hobsbawm as "Heaneyspeak ... the snap-crackle-and-pop of diction".

The less self-conscious language of 'Cow in Calf', for example, clearly embodies a pragmatic, down-to-earth attitude to the birth: "It seems she has swallowed a barrel"; "her belly is slung like a hammock." The comparison with inanimate objects distances the poet — and the reader — from the animal. The attitude towards the cow is the practical one of the farmer, not the sentimental one of the city dweller.

But in terms of reclaiming the past, it is important to notice that throughout his poetry Heaney's use of language seems more Celtic than English. Nowhere is this more evident than in the place-name poems. As Elmer Andrews has pointed out, in these poems, "language is pushed towards a magical relationship with the things it is speaking about".[10] They demonstrate that Heaney could use English to express "a sensibility conditioned by belonging to a particular place, an ancestry, a history, a culture, that was not English".[11] While Heaney felt he could produce "erotic mouth-music by and out of the Anglo-Saxon tongue" and still be faithful to his "own non-English origins", it has to be said that the "erotic mouth-music" is an Irish rather than an English phenomenon with at least some roots in the poetic nature of the Irish language. 'Broagh' ('riverbank'), echoing the sound of rain, contains one of the residual sounds of the Irish language — gh — while 'Anahorish' suggests the landscape it describes: "soft gradient / of consonant, vowel-meadow".

Of course, it is impossible to consider Heaney's language without discussing his increasing concern with myth, history and the political and social divisions of Northern Ireland. Issues of language and culture in his work, together with the notions of hegemony and cultural stratification discussed so far, become increasingly complex, evinced particularly, and problematically, in *North*.

The immediate literary antecedent for Heaney's *North* is the work of John Montague with which the North, as Seamus

Deane maintains, became the "crucial territory in Irish poetry".[12] In Montague's poetry, the real, local Tyrone and the older mythological past, what he calls 'Ancient Ireland', are fused in an attempt to deal with the breakdown of Irish, national, Gaelic culture through the increasing violence of Ulster.

The themes of breakdown and discontinuity are much stronger in Irish than in Welsh poetry. Though both cultures — Welsh and Gaelic — have been colonised, the history, and the patterns of subjection have been very different. What has happened in Ireland, observed from Wales, as in Clarke's 'Fires on Llŷn', by some writers as a course of events to be feared, has set poetry and history in a special kind of relationship. As Seamus Deane has argued: the chief characteristic of modern Irish poetry is "the confrontation between poetry as a system of order and history as a spectacle of disorder".[13]

However, in his preoccupation with history in *North* ,Heaney has a number of other mentors, too, not the least of which is Thomas Kinsella. Not only do they both demonstrate "the recurrent tendency of Irish poetry to avail of antiquarian and historical research into the past", but they both develop an increasing concern with "the incorporation of that which is repellent and disintegrated for the sake of a more comprehensive system of order in which the disorder will be subsumed."[14]

North has attracted harsh criticism as well as acclaim. Morrison describes it as one of the most depressing of Heaney's books, attributing the bleakness to the author's fatalism and to the image of the "North" itself as "an arctic cul-de-sac from which one can escape only by turning round and going south".[15] But it has to be seen as the culmination of some of the major trends and developments of Heaney's early work. Indeed, even Morrison accepts that it is Heaney's "most concerted effort to interpret the tragic history of Ulster" impelled by "the conviction that the structures of feeling may slowly be changed".[16]

The overt mythical and symbolic nature of *North* has caused most unease. So much so, that Falck finds the direct, documentary approach of Part II a relief after the myth of Part I.[17] Of course, the Troubles present special problems for Irish poets. On one level, literature and the arts seem incapable of coping with the reality of the Troubles, while, on another, writers who try to do so risk charges of being exploitative. Deane has gone so far as to argue that the traditional myths should be abandoned in favour of a compromise between the imaginative and "the brute facts of the public world".

A number of critics have also expressed unease over Heaney's concern with the idyllic and the rural, and even if his myths contain "no heroicising impulse" he does seem caught on a contracting threshold.[19] Indeed, Longley feels that Heaney risks glamorising the conflict: "determinism, the plundering of the past for parallels, circular thinking (all incidentally features of Republican and Loyalist ideology) once more insist on 'territorial piety', on a religious-anthropological, even slightly glamorous way of apprehending the conflict."[20]

The method of *North*, too, has attracted criticism. Longley believes that it is less successful than that of *Wintering Out* because it appears "fascinated more by bones, fossils, relics, archaism" than "by those things which they are emblems of"; because "an obsession with stacking up parallels, has replaced flexible soundings"; and because "the contracted or 'perfected' perception of the Bog People in *North* renders their emblematic functions, as well as his poetry, less complex."[21]

These features of Heaney's poetry are actually among those which David Greene has identified as signifying the decay of myth.[22] Heaney, if we accept Longley's verdict, finds himself in the situation described by Greene "in which a poet will pick up some pieces of the myth of the past, what was a coherent and unifying force, and use them for poetic purposes."[23] All the criticisms do not detract from the serious attempt in *North* to rediscover and reclaim a coherent, cultural past and a fulfilling identity in the present. Indeed, the search for continuities, going back into the past to discover lines of direction, is central to *North*, as Anthony Thwaite argues:

> the message was one of continuity, established right from the beginning in the two dedicatory poems ... and going on through the bog corpses, the Viking invaders, the English massacres, an English journalist in search of "views / On the Irish thing" to the "Inner émigré" the poet sees himself as having become, "a wood-kerne / Escaped from the massacre."[24]

64

In Heaney's work we have, as Curtis has said, a "slow process of politicisation"[25] so that only eventually does he speak out as a member of a disadvantaged minority in Northern Ireland: a Catholic and a Republican. Confronting the fact that

> a generation who lived by violence, who could only live, express their sense of nationality, find fulfilment, through violence, was baptised in the Easter Rising and the bloody Civil War six years later in 1922.[26]

The political dimension of his work, then, only gradually acquired depth and sophistication, evident, for example, in even a cursory comparison of 'Docker' and 'The Other Side'. The latter is a recreation of the divided community in which the poet grew up, which as Longley says, politicises the terrain.[27] The increasing complexity of Heaney's world-view is evident in the way in which even here Catholicism itself, the ritual that excludes the protestant farmer, is seen as rather tired and exhausted compared with the vigour of Protestantism. And it is a complex poem in another sense too. As Longley has pointed out, while "the price of grass-seed" in the poem symbolises "the costs of fundamental growth and change", the poem itself "symbolises the cross-fertilisation between poets and traditions in Ulster".[28]

The increasingly complex view of identity complicates also the notions of resistance we discussed earlier. Longley argues that "empathy with one Ulster community, such as Heaney's in *North*, might constrain rather than release a poet's imagination".[29] Acknowledging "the intensive pressure on Heaney, including his own sense of duty: to be more Irish, to be more political", she detects that what in the early work is immediate and painful is stylised and distanced in the later work and, what was original as a "form of procedure" becomes "a less original form of content ('imperial power' versus 'territorial piety')..."[30].

The elegy for his cousin Colum McCartney, who was shot by terrorists in County Armagh, in *Field Work*, ends with Heaney imaginatively cleaning and laying out the body — traditionally, female tasks. By implication, the rôle of poetry is to cleanse and liberate:

I turn because the sweeping of your feet
Has stopped behind me, to find you on your knees
With blood and roadside muck in your hair and eyes,
Then kneel in front of you in brimming grass
And gather up cold handfuls of the dew
To wash you, cousin. I dab you clean with moss
Fine as the drizzle out of a low cloud.
I lift you under the arms and lay you flat.
With rushes that shoot green again, I plait
Green scapulars to wear over your shroud.

The lines are riddled with religious connotations and shot through with tenderness and love. It is not Heaney at his best, however, because so much is evaded.

In *Station Island* , ironically, Colum's ghost arraigns Heaney for prettifying death with poetry instead of avenging it. This tension between the poet and the man-of-action which we find in most of Heaney's collections, emblematic in Heaney's case of the failure to engage satisfactorily with the political present, is felt by other poets, even outside of Ireland, as was suggested in Part One.

'The Harvest Bow' in *Field Work* presents a solution similar to that which Harrison arrives at in the latter part of *V*, where Harrison is arraigned by his alter ego for "prettifying" in poetry what has happened to the working class. The bow, made by Heaney's father, is an example of the skill that belongs to an older, rural Ireland, and a symbol of continuity, of ancestral kinship with the land, and of a deeply felt sense of love and belonging. It is, then, an artefact which has a social function — as a symbol of love, continuity, order — which poetry also can assume and as such it anticipates the haw lantern in the later collection.

Admittedly, Heaney fails to employ this perspective in a satisfactory engagement with the politics of murder and concentration camps. Heaney's 'From the Canton of Expectation' in *The Haw Lantern* remembers:

Once a year we gathered in a field
of dance platforms and tents where children sang
songs they learned by rote in the old language.

There is a passivity here — not only are the songs in "the old language", but they are "learned by rote" — which is also to be found in the account of how "we turned for home and the usual, harassment / by militiamen on overtime at roadblocks." It stands in contrast to the new "grammar / of imperatives, the new age of demands". At first, the new spirit is presented as if it were something to be admired for it enlivens "young heads that might have dozed a life away / against the flanks of milking cows..." But the fact that the poet resents what has happened in social and political terms is especially evident in his anger over what is happening to language: "They would banish the conditional for ever /this generation born impervious to /the triumph in our cries of *de profundis*." Heaney can no more follow them than Tony Harrison can follow the impervious skinheads with their aerosol cans in *V*. In *The Haw Lantern*, Heaney listens for a sound amidst the uproar that will tell him of one man still alive and committed to imagination: "who stood his ground in the indicative, / whose boat will lift when the cloudburst happens."

The haw lantern itself is a symbol of an imaginative holism that transcends the history and personal imagination antithesis of *North* and *Station Island* and finds freedom from the earlier determinism. But this imaginative holism risks retreat into an idealised past disconnected from the political present. It would be a distortion, however, to see *The Haw Lantern*'s championing of the imaginative, transcendence of language over the determinism of history as a radical departure from the previous works. In *The Haw Lantern*, there is a shift in emphasis which is best understood in the light of what is present, albeit less prominently, in the poetry that preceded it and is especially present where Heaney opposes in his poetry the masculine and the feminine.

III

As Tony Curtis argues: Heaney has always approached the Troubles "from the rural context which is his birthright".[31] Notwithstanding the political decision of moving South, Curtis suggests that Heaney is advocating in his poetry [written before *The*

Haw Lantern] that "for peace to return to Ulster the people have to re-establish the rhythm of the natural world".[32] However, there is more to it than this even in *North* and *Fieldwork*. Heaney is interested in the cultural holism which he finds in rural Ireland — the heart of Irish-language culture.

Of course, looking back to try to find a sense of holism in Irish life is commonplace in Irish poetry. In Austin Clarke's work, for example, monastic life becomes a metaphor for the integrated culture. Anglo-Celts are inevitably haunted by the fact that they have been robbed of what is their rightful cultural inheritance. So much so, that Parts I and II of Heaney's *North* are not as completely opposed to each other as some critics have suggested. According to Hooker, the poems in "Part II show the poetry confronting the destructive forces unloosed by a particular social and political crisis, but without using the regenerative myth that encompasses his [Heaney's] earlier treatment of the same theme".[33] Both Part I and Part II, however, have to be seen against a sense of a past encapsulated in the introductory poems where everyday objects supply the imagery which speaks of a meaningful, self-fulfilling, holistic life. Hence, Heaney's aunt, for example, in the first introductory poem is representative of a holism which Heaney sees as an essential ingredient of the Celtic cultural past in which men and women were not alienated from their work, from their environment and from the product of their labour.

One of the most successful critics to have penetrated the concern with holism in Irish poetry, Seamus Deane, writing from the perspective of an Irishman, concludes: "our present dilapidated situation has borne in upon us more fiercely than ever the fact that discontinuity ... is more truly the signal feature of our condition."[34]

The lure of the tribal past, the period before dispossession, for Heaney as for many Irish poets has to be seen within this broad context. Tribal punishment could be harsh, the product of a communality which had little truck with individualism. As an intelligent, sensitive humanitarian Heaney is aware of this. But he is also able to feel the sense of belonging; the security in one's cultural roots; the sense of working for, and contributing to, a culture that is alive and active that constituted this past, in which the association with land was important as a symbol of cultural continuity.

It is not coincidental that the first of the two dedicatory poems which establish the message of *North* and which introduce the major themes of the collection, is not only dedicated to, but based upon a memory of, Heaney's aunt. What is remembered is as much a part of the country's cultural past as the poet's familial past and it is significant for the collection as a whole, for its delving into the past after ancestral lines and continuities, that the guardian of the first custom we encounter, of the home and the family, of love and a sense of belonging, is a woman. The imagery of sunlight as a griddle and water as honey encloses the poem in a kind of "domestic holism". In this respect *North* is unlike *Death of a Naturalist* which opens with a memory of his father. While 'Digging' closes with a comparison of the poet's pen with a spade, this poem closes with a tin shovel as symbolic of love.

IV

The way in which the masculine and the feminine are opposed in Heaney's poetry has been underemphasised by critics yet any consideration of it immediately exposes the, albeit changing, dynamic between culture, ancestry and identity in his work and the central place which it occupies. The contrast between Heaney's aunt's hands scuffing over the bakeboard, dusting it with a goose's wing, in the first dedicatory poem of *North*, and the hands of the seedcutters holding knives in the second dedicatory poem recalls 'The Wife's Tale' in the earlier collection, *Door into the Dark*. In that poem, there is a similar contrast between the sensitivity of the woman's hands and the way in which the men are associated with violence through the seed which is like shot, the field which is a "battlefield" and the pitchforks which are "javelins". Of course, hands, among the most expressive parts of the body, traditionally signify strength and providence and, in a religious country, blessing. Also, traditionally, the goose as an attribute of the earth god, suggests love and in this respect both anticipate the image which concludes the first dedicatory poem and reinforces the special significance of the

female:
> And here is love
> like a tinsmith's scoop.
> Sunk past its gleam
> in the meal-bin.

Mary Heaney is recalled not only for herself, but as a representative of all Irish women and mothers. In Irish poetry, women and the feminine sensibility have a particular force: signifying the Great Mother, Ireland herself, self-assuaging and self-sustaining. In this respect, the cultural framework of historically-determined meanings in which Heaney seeks orientation is left unchallenged.

Heaney himself has drawn attention to the way Catholicism attuned his sensibility toward the feminine:

> The reality that was addressed was maternal, and the posture was
> one of supplication. Irish Catholicism, until about ten years ago,
> had this Virgin Mary Worship, almost Worship. In practice, the
> shrines, the rosary beads, all the devotions were centred towards
> a feminine presence, which I think was terrific for the sensibility.[36]

Not surprisingly, then, *North* develops a concept from 'Undine' in *Door into the Dark* where the speaker of the poem, a female water spirit that seeps into and nourishes the farmer's soil, signifies the union between the (male) farmer and his land. Part I of *North* begins and ends with, is framed by, the myth of Antaeus, son of Poseidon and Mother Earth. The focus in the first poem is upon Antaeus' proximity with the earth: in his boast that he "cannot be weaned / Off the earth's long contour, her river-veins", the implicit reference to Mother Earth is unmistakable and it is developed later in Antaeus' confession:

> I am cradled in the dark that wombed me
> And nurtured in every artery
> Like a small hillock.

In Heaney's poetry, as in Gillian Clarke's, the feminine sensibility is coterminous with a sympathetic appreciation of nature. The Germanic rituals from the peat bogs are significant for Heaney as expressions of a sensibility that was nurtured in the past by a life lived in contact with nature. When Heaney says "we pine for ceremony, / customary rhythms", the qualification of ceremony as customs linked with natural rhythms is pertinent. In fact, this sensibility is partly responsible for the difference between 'The Tollund Man' and the later poem, 'The Grabaulle Man'. 'The Grabaulle Man', Longley points out, has an "air of contemplation", of "ritual observance", and of resurrection: "the chain of intensive similes reinforces the point that the man has been translated into the element of the bog and is thus at one with faintly healing Nature".[37]

The opposition of a male and female sensibility, rooted in rather stereotypical gender assumptions, is important in a number of the poems in *North*. The rather voyeuristic nature of 'Punishment' to which Morrison rightly draws attention should not blind us to the way in which the poem develops the analogy, briefly stated at the end of 'The Grauballe Man', between the IRA and the Iron Age in the complicitous reference there to the "hooded victim, / slashed and dumped". As Morrison says: the girl's "tar-black" face and shaved head link her with "the betraying sisters" of present-day Northern Ireland, Catholic girls who have been shaved, tarred and feathered by the IRA as a punishment for informing upon or "going out" with British soldiers.[39] Despite its uncomfortable armchair voyeurism, the poem is a powerful exploration and exposure of the poet's ambivalence: of how, despite his humanitarian concern for the woman as a victim, he would "have stood dumb" understanding "the exact/ and tribal, intimate revenge". Heaney himself saw the North as essentially male. In 'The Betrothal of Cavehill', he writes of it as "proud, protestant and northern and male" and, in the *Irish Times* (1975), lamented that "a poet cannot influence events in the North because it is the men of action that are influencing everybody and everything."

We have already noted how, in the introductory poems of *North*, as in 'The Wife's Tale', despite being one of the poems most critical of stereotypical gender roles, women are associated with love and domestic calm, but the men are connected with violence. The same opposition underpins 'After a Killing', the first of the 'Triptych' poems in which Heaney is struggling, as Elmer Andrews says, to hold on to his faith.[40] This poem, written after the murder of the British Ambassador to Ireland,

Christopher Ewart-Biggs, in 1976, contrasts the sinister, night-marish men with rifles and a young girl at Heaney's own coast-al home carrying a basket of vegetables. The girl here represents the female principle of bearing and is the simulacrum of a fu-ture beyond the terror and the violence. It is a faith that at times becomes rather shaky: even though a woman in 'A Drink of Water' is eventually able to provide a drink — the poet has "dipped to drink again to be / Faithful" — she has grown old, "Like an old bat staggering up the Field."

The women in Heaney's poetry are often sensuous. In 'The Wife's Tale', for example, the woman judges the seed by the way it feels in her hand. But they are often also controlled by the men as the wife in 'The Wife's Tale' who cuts her husband's bread as he likes it and uncomplainingly obeys his order to test the potato seeds. The square of cloth is a symbol of her realm of influence and, as Elmer Andrews says, "a genteel miniature of the rough square of field the men work."[41] Her isolation is rein-forced by the complicitous wink which she notices passing be-tween the men:

> Heaney's probing of the relationship between the sexes discloses in intimate detail the way the woman's life is determined by the man; and the revelation of her sensitive awareness co-existing with acceptance of her condition, without protest, without rancour, is no small triumph of intuition and finesse.[42]

This is the whole colonial situation in which Ireland finds it-self in microcosm and which throughout Heaney's poetry is portrayed in terms of female subjection and male domination. In 'Act of Union' the sexual connotations are obvious:

> Your back is a firm line of eastern coast
> And arms and legs are thrown
> Beyond your gradual hills. I caress
> The heaving province where our past has grown.

Here, the poem, as Longley says, in "pursuing the parallel be-tween sexual and political union, and between imperialism and maleness, ends up with the speaker guiltily fathering Ulster Unionism."[43]

In developing the male-female opposition of *North* in a

broader political context, Heaney casts his net wider than Ireland. While 'Antaeus' is written from the point of view of Antaeus, his overthrow in the later poem, 'Hercules and Antaeus', is told in the third person reinforcing his dispossession. For the defeat of Antaeus is not just the overthrow of Ireland, portrayed in 'Ocean's Love to Ireland' as a rape, but symbolically of all minority cultures: "Balor will die / and Byrthnoth and Sitting Bull." The "remorseless V" which Hercules makes with his arms in lifting Antaeus above his head indicates victory, but also the familiar gesture of defiance. As the sign for 'versus' it also suggests, however, perpetual conflict.

It hardly needs pointing out that in some of his poetry the myth of the female, of Mother Earth, is developed by Heaney in a direction that is much darker than anything we find in, for example, Gillian Clarke's poetry. 'Bog Queen', Longley points out, "has the advantage of dealing directly with the goddess herself, so that questionable behaviour on the part of her acolytes may be ignored."[44] But, of course, the concepts of Mother Earth and sacrifice are concomitant. Heaney said himself in 'Mother Ireland' (*The Listener*, 7 December, 1972): "You have a society in the Iron Age where there was a ritual blood-letting. You have a society where girls' heads were shaved for adultery, you have a religion centring on the territory, on a goddess of the ground, and of the land, and associated with sacrifice."

Sacrifice, encapsulating the birth, death and rebirth cycle through the restoration of fertility to the land, signifies the restoration of primordial unity. In sacrifice, the sacrificer and sacrificed become one — signifying the unity and duality of the universe.

The interest in ritual and the restoration of a promordial unity which accompanies it has a special appeal in the face of what appears to be the "inconclusiveness", to employ Edna Longley's term, of Irish culture and history. Thus, Heaney suggests, tentatively, that the Tollund Man's union with the Earth Goddess evinces a transfiguring process applicable to the Troubles. But the concept of sacrifice is a problematic one to apply to the reality of contemporary Northern Ireland. No sooner do we start to rediscover ritual, customary rhythms and the tribal origins of Celtic culture, than we come up against a reality that is darker, more brutal and even bloodier: "the goddess swallows / our love and terror."

While *North* is successful in trying to put the violence of Northern Ireland into a wider perspective — essential for the poet to understand his rôle as a poet as opposed to a man of action — it fails to achieve a Yeatsian vision encompassing beauty and atrocity. The reality cannot be gainsaid as 'Orange Drums, Tyrone, 1966', for example, testifies. Its seemingly imprecise imagery — the air "pounding like a stethoscope" and drums compared with giant, cancerous tumours — embody in themselves the violence they are meant to convey, the effect that such a parade would have upon a Catholic minority within earshot.

Perhaps the imaginative field of *North* is too large for Heaney to map adequately. *Field Work*, underpinned by his move to County Wicklow and the return to close contact with nature, has its imaginative sights set much closer, trained on an area the size of a field. The title poem focuses upon a woman, his wife, as the means by which opposites are synthesized into a larger holism. The vaccination mark on her arm is both an innoculation and a wound. Metamorphosed as a dryad, she encompasses the world of opposites within herself and mirrors nature: she is both nurturing/mothering and diseased (ring wormed). The central symbol of the poem is the circle — an image of perfection, continuance and healing.

Part II of 'Fieldwork' concludes with the cyclic images of the moon, overhanging them both, and of the coin on the Pequod's mast — signifying the fusion of the masculine and feminine — which are opposed, as Elmer Andrews points out, to the linear movement of the train, on the way to the slaughter house, that temporarily comes between them at the end of Part 1.[45] What emerges here — encapsulated later by the leaf which Heaney presses into his loved one's hand, thereby staining her — is an acceptance of disfigurement and perfection as opposing aspects of the same reality. Achieving a confidence in the idealism of his vocation which he was unable to muster convincingly in *North* (in, for example, 'Exposure'), Heaney discovers a holism which always finally eluded him in the earlier collections. The antithetical images associated with circles and lines throughout

'Fieldwork' are most convincingly fused in the key image of the sunflower which has a sunlike circle at its heart and is joined to the earth by a long stem. In Heaney's poem, the sunflower is braced to the pebble-dashed wall, suggesting that the flower achieves freedom and perfection while accepting, as Andrews argues, the restraints and regularities of Earth.[46] The fusion of the vertical, suggesting the masculine, with the circle, signifying the feminine, perfection, and closure, is a synthesis on a number of levels: personal, domestic, marital, artistic, psychic, political and cultural. But at the political level, it is unsatisfactory. It suggests, but does not achieve, a synthesis which a number of other contemporary poets concerned with similar issues of culture and identity have also been unable to achieve. Ironically, their strengths and originalities as writers would have been less if they had done so.

Like many of his contemporaries, Heaney is at his best in tackling issues of culture and identity when the local rather than the nation or even region is made the locus of discussion. In this respect, *Seeing Things* is an inevitable development. In its concern with childhood, it appears, on a cursory reading, less political than the approach taken in 'A Constable Calls' from the second part of *North* and even in the early work. But in these poems Heaney reveals his recurring concern to construct an identity upon a locality that transcends the boundaries of a particular, geographical place and bypasses, even subverts, notions of nationalism and hegemony. The development of his work through *Seeing Things* encourages us to look at Irish and Northern Irish poetry in terms of smaller units such as localities and, as we have suggested and will see in the next chapter, the same may be said of Welsh writing as well.

CHAPTER FOUR

IGNITING PENT SILENCES: GILLIAN CLARKE, SALLY ROBERTS JONES AND OLIVER REYNOLDS

Being Anglo - *any* thing is really tough;
any gaps you can fill with sighs.

And get some roots, juggle names like
Taliesin and ap Gwilym.
          John Davies ('How to Write Anglo-Welsh Poetry')

new voices must rise,
for Wales cannot endlessly remain
chasing sheep into the twilight.
          Peter Finch ('A Welsh Wordscape')

I

In the previous chapter, we saw Heaney's highly politicised concern with his past — familial, social and national — and with the historically-determined present of Northern Ireland inextricably entwined with this past. In pursuing the key issues raised in the previous chapters with more detailed reference to three, very different English-language, Welsh writers, we are concerned to show how once again a sharp focus upon ancestry, culture and identity brings us close to the creative centre of many of the works and to the particular dynamic in each case between author, text and reader.

Much of the chapter is concerned with Gillian Clarke, who in a relatively short space of time, has won considerable critical acclaim. Her work is not as obviously as politicised as that of Heaney or some of the North of England poets discussed in chapter two. It is political at a profound level and, as we shall see, overtly challenges, unlike Heaney's work, the gender stereotypes within the historically determined cultural framework in which she, as much as Heaney, seeks orientation and definition.

Clarke's first love is rural Wales and it would be easy, as some critics have done, to shoehorn her work into the tradition of Welsh, English-language writing about a disappearing rural past. Yet it is a line of enquiry which, like the comparison of her work to that of R.S. Thomas, in whose footsteps she literally walks in 'Fires on Llŷn', is of limited value. Focusing instead upon Clarke as a woman who, as a poet, is concerned with articulating the history and experience of what it means to be a woman, highlights the originality of her contribution to Welsh writing in English.

Before considering Clarke's concern, from the perspective of a woman, with her cultural and familial ancestry, it is important for the full understanding of her poetry to highlight, albeit briefly, how her feminine sensibility is revealed through the symbolism of her works. In particular, in some poems there is concern with the "feminine principle" of holding opposites together. For example, rain and sun: white roses that bloom after rain hold "water and sunlight"; buckets hold spring water and late summer heat; rain and late sun glisten "in brimful leaves". Or heat and cold occur together signifying life and death: in 'Curlew' the poet's scythe reduces the cantref to "the heart / of eggs in the cold grass". Moreover as Hooker has said, "her fertile images contain death, her images of death hold seeds of life."[1]

In the early poems, there is a sense of time and mortality which suggests a dark side to Clarke's work. In favouring a concluding line that points to the future, many of her early poems close ominously. 'Baby-sitting', where Clarke envisages the child asking and demanding "milk-familiar comforting", concludes: "it will not come. It will not come." 'Sunday' ends with the poet admitting "a warning I can't name". Even 'Harvest at Mynachlog' has a Hardyesque ending:

We are quiet again, holding our cups
In turn for the tilting milk, sad, hearing
The sun roar like a rush of grain
Engulfing all winged things that live

One moment in the eclipsing light.

But in the poetry as a whole the melancholy is usually curbed, as Jeremy Hooker suggests.[2] We can see the way that "she wins her affirmations from the strong pull of death" in the above passage from 'Harvest at Mynachlog', in the references to "cup" and "tilting milk" which provide a backloth to the melancholic note on which the poem closes. Symbolically "cup" and "milk" suggest life and the female. And, not surprisingly, the realisation of life as a process comes to the fore at the end also of 'Birth': we have "the signal / Of milk's incoming tide, and satisfaction / Fall like a clean sheet around us." The "incoming tide" here contrasts positively with the "incoming night" of the first verse.

The sensibility underpinning this symbolism is evident also in those poems which consciously reach back to the past. 'Login' is concerned with a visit which the poet makes with her son to a house where her father once lived. The poem opens by listing key features of the village. Chapel and bridge come first. The bridge signifies what connects the poet to her past. But the fourth feature mentioned is "a river running fast" which "divides the wild cow parsley". Here again the poem may be read both literally and symbolically. For the river divides not only the cow parsley, but signifies the separation of the poet from this particular aspect of her past. It is only after the mention of the river that we have the words in which the poet asks about her father. The old lady stands in the dark passage of her house and as they talk the sun moves over her, lifting the shadow. The "passage" is both the literal hallway of the house and the past in which the old woman has lived and still lives. The poet is the present needing to make connections with the past as much as the dark passage needs to have the light enter. After the talk over tea both women, past and present standing together, watch the poet's son, signifying the future, running into the light. The final image is of the bridge brilliant with sunlight, signifying the completion of the "bridge-building" process. For the boy a kind of baptism has occurred of which he is not yet aware. The old lady has "ruffled" the boy's brown hair with "a hand / that is bruised with age". The ageing hand on the boy's young, growing head is a symbolic baptism of him

into time, while the word "ruffles" suggests how the boy's innocence will be disturbed as he grows up into an awareness of
mortality. The poem closes on a note of melancholy with the
poet imagining how, should the boy turn and wave, he'd "hear
footsteps / not yet taken fade away."

Joining the present with the past is an important concept in
Clarke's poetry not unrelated to the "feminine principle" of
holding opposites together. In describing the motivation behind
'Letter from a Far Country', Clarke has said:

> When you write like that, you release something that's actually
> pretty deeply within your memory and imagination. And by writ-
> ing something long instead of the usual short, shaped, forged thing
> that I had been writing, I realized that digging deep was an import-
> ant way forward for me. Going into the past, going deeper, going
> down through the layers became important. I was mining my own
> memory, my family's memory and Welsh memory as far as I could,
> within the restrictions of a half-hour poem. That's more important
> to me. That is how I am writing now, because the past informs what
> we are now.[3]

Mining her own memory, her family's memory and the Welsh
memory are obviously central to 'Cofiant' from *Letting in the
Rumour* (1989), based on the Welsh nineteenth-century tradition
of writing biography. The poem is a combination of personal
recollection, family lore, anecdote, and historical research:

> Houses we've lived in
> inhabit us
> and history's restless
> in the rooms of the mind.

But the regard for the past expressed here overtly informs
some of Clarke's shorter poems, too, especially 'Jac Codi Baw', a
poem which can be discussed as an interesting comparison with
Anne Stevenson's 'Demolition' from *The Fiction-Makers*. Anne
Stevenson is a poet for whom Clarke has a high regard. She has
admitted how "in one sense, the woman writer begins to write
coming across Sylvia Plath, Anne Sexton, Anne Stevenson..."[4]
and has dedicated 'Epithalamium' to her.

What emerges from 'Jac Codi Baw' and 'Demolition', almost
by default, is an image of the statue-of-identity holding the
scales of progress in which the 'past' and the 'present', 'demoli-

tion' and 'preservation', are in equal balance. I say 'by default' because each of these poems presents us with what Clarke in another poem, echoing Yeats, describes as "some terrible undoing".

'Jac Codi Baw' — a local Welsh-language nickname for a J.C.B., literally meaning as Clarke explains in an end note, 'Jack dig the dirt'[5] — begins with contrasts in time: a contrast between the time it has taken to tear down the building with the time the building has stood and the time it has taken her, as a shopper, to fill a shopping bag. The speed of the demolition is further contrasted with the change that weather brings, the gradual demise of a generation, and the slow crumbling of a building:

> They have torn down in the space of time
> it takes to fill a shopping bag,
> the building that stood beside my car.
> It was grown over with ragwort,
> toad flax and buddleia, windows
> blind with boarding....
> .... We are used to the slow
> change that weather brings, the gradual
> death of a generation, old bricks
> crumbling.

The poet returns to find her car covered in dust and the driver of the great machine treating the whole episode as a joke. The positioning of the woman here as victim of the male J.C.B. driver's insensitivity is rooted in the kind of scenario, however stereotypical, which many women will recognise. But there is more to the incident than this. The poem contrasts the indifference, and in this case, masculine and mechanised will-to-change, with the feminine sensibility which is sensitive to the past and which in this poem is both literally and metaphorically ridden roughshod over. While the sensibility epitomised by the J.C.B. and its driver has a ruthless indifference to the past, the feminine sensibility has more of an awareness of what is destroyed in the destruction of buildings as Clarke's last phrase, "Blood on our hands" suggests, in a rather sensational overstatement.

Anne Stevenson's 'Demolition' begins, like Clarke's 'Jac Codi Baw', with an anonymous 'they'. Again the demolition is wrought by a machine, in this case, a digger, personified as a monstrous head with "yellow fangs slavering rubble and purple brickdust". As in Clarke's poem, the will-to-destroy is contrasted with an aesthetic appreciation of the bridge rooted in an awareness of the part it has played in the lives of so many generations. The former sees an "old brick bridge / connecting the coal works with the coke works." The language is economical, functional like the bridge. The stress is on the bridge's part in a process: coal to coke. But the latter sensibility sees:

> it was ever a chapel of small waters,
> a graceful arch toothworked with
> yellow bricks notched into red bricks.

Suddenly, there are graceful, curved lines and colour, traditionally and significantly associated with the feminine, not the straight lines and grey traditionally associated with a masculine sensibility. In our attitude towards the past, towards death, is our attitude towards life. The watchers wear "grave" expressions, as well they might, for as the poem says, exploiting the pun, "they might be grieving".

Anne Stevenson's 'Demolition' is one of a number of poems, the 'Black Grate Poems', dedicated to the way of life that grew up around coal and written in the face of a modern sensibility that would forget it ever existed. In her creation of a sense of a working past in these poems, Anne Stevenson shares a purpose with poets such as Robert Minhinnick: "a poet of worked historical place: of quarries, for example, or docks, or derelict industrial sites, or a former large estate — all places on his 'native ground' in South Wales."[6] But Stevenson is distinguishable from poets, such as Minhinnick, by her awareness of the contrast between a masculine and feminine sensibility which she has in common with Clarke.

The contrast between the masculine and feminine sensibility displayed in different attitudes to the past underpins many poems by both Clarke and Stevenson. In Clarke's 'Cardiff Elms', which concerns the destruction of these magnificent trees by Dutch elm disease, the description of the elms in their heyday once again betrays a feminine sensibility. Their leaves are seen as lace, they stretch over a rose-coloured road, and they cast fingering shadows. Their rôle is seen in traditionally feminine terms: as protective, sheltering. Without them the city's Civic Centre is bolder and open to the burning sun.

The perspective on time taken in 'Letter from a Far Country' and *The Fiction-Makers* is profoundly similar and essentially feminine. Both Clarke and Stevenson challenge the illusion of past, present and future: Clarke with quiet determination; Stevenson with a sense of one who has suddenly come alive to new perspectives. As Stevenson says: "I am eight and eighteen and eighty all the Augusts of my day." Indeed, to think of the present and/or the future without due reference to the past is an unnatural perspective. Both poets argue that we have to return to the feminine to correct our wayward, masculine arrogance.

Stevenson, unlike Clarke, is not so much concerned with the role of men and women as such, but with the way in which it is not the feminine intelligence, with its respect for the past and a caring, protective sensibility, that has shaped civilisation, but the more masculine will which finds expression in weapons of war and turns the world to its own ends. The poem, 'The Fiction-Makers', turns the traditional biblical story of the creation of women from men on its head for it is the "feminine principle", the dark secret womb of the earth that gives birth to, and nurtures, the masculine. Yet it almost has to be born. It pulls at her. It is a will full of hunger.

If Stevenson in this poem dwells on this masculine aspect and touches on the rôle of women, Clarke concentrates on the rôle of women and touches on the aggression in the male will:

> If we go hunting along with the men
> Who will light the fires and bake bread then?
> Who'll catch the nightmares and ride them away
> If we put to sea and we sail away?
>
> Will the men grow tender and the children strong?
> Who will teach the Mam iaith and sing them songs?
> If we adventure more than a day
> Who will do the loving while we're away?

'In Pisgah Graveyard', the words "Er Côf" ('In Memoriam') trigger off the sense of the culture in which the poet's ancestral roots are buried, both literally and metaphorically. She begins to empathise with their lives, her own ancestral past, as she imagines their lives and families. The poem is informed by the same awareness as that which underpins 'Cofiant' and 'Letter from a Far Country' where, in describing her grandmother hanging out the sheets, the lapse into Welsh signifies the closeness of the bond she now feels with her ancestors: "Mamgu's best pais. Her Sunday frock." The word "Mamgu" is warm, spontaneous, loving. John Penri Williams' last Welsh words to his daughter — "Hwyl fawr, Cariad" — acquire an equally strategic emphasis — although they are obviously more poignant — in the English-language narrative about him in 'Cofiant'.

The sense of empathy Clarke feels with the past, even in her early work, is concomitant with inheriting a sense of Wales, especially rural Wales. 'In Pisgah Graveyard' identifies the two dimensions of Dewi Emrys' life: the earth and the chapel:

> And all around the living corn concedes
> Fecundity to him. They're proud of him
> Here, where full barns count as much as poetry
> He, who, they say, knew women as well as words,
> Lies in the blond fields blowing to seed
> With the threshing machine and the chapel clock.

The sensual aspect of Emrys' life is handled with grace, tact and a wry humour. The famous poet's success with women is juxtaposed with his skill with words and in turn linked with the fertilising powers of his rotting body after his death. We have the impression of an earthy, physical yet spiritual man who was somehow larger-than-life, lived an irregular life, and yet earned the respect of his community because he was a bard. Here Clarke is trying to get behind the name, behind the gravestone, even behind the language, or perhaps one should say inside the language, not only to understand, but feel this man's culture and sensibility:

> What do I look for here, with a child's
> Hot hand in mine, his hair like ragged robin?
> Perhaps the stone words of my first tongue
> On a poet's grave that tidies his wild life,
> For the savage roar of the trapped sun
> Seeding the earth against the stop of winter
> ....
> The words unfreeze and the poems come again.

Appreciation of that former life, the rediscovery of her ancestral roots, becomes a spur to creativity. There is a sense of process, of wholeness.

Envisaging what it was that impelled the lives of her Welsh ancestors is important also in another poem. This time the title, 'Storm Awst', is itself in the Welsh language:

> Will the tyddyn,
> In its group of strong trees on the high
> Hill, hold against the storm Awst
> Running across hills where everything
> Alive listens, pacing its house, heart still?

A 'tyddyn' was a unit, in the Welsh rural, social structure, just as the August storms had a special place in the experiences and sensibilities of the rural Welsh farmers. If it were called 'August Storm' the force of the poem would be lost. The 'Storm Awst' lives in the Welsh rural folklore and is peculiar to Wales. Knowing it, expecting it and coping with it reflects a knowledge passed down from one generation to another, all of whom have lived in the same place and in the same culture. The rediscovering of this lore, of this knowledge, has to do with looking at Wales as a Welsh person. Of course, there is another important theme here for Welsh culture, that of resistance and resilience.

It is this Welsh dimension of 'Storm Awst' that separates it from a similar poem, 'Wind', by Ted Hughes. Both poems have a similar elemental awareness and fear of the storm. But Clarke's poem with its reference to local lore and sayings ("The gypsies are making their fires" is a saying which refers to puffs of mist over woods, presaging rain) brings to the fore the sensibility of the rural Welsh who are able to achieve a deep-rooted, almost physical, knowledge of their environment. Gillian Clarke has herself admitted how Welsh-language culture influenced her:

> As I began to read Welsh poetry in translation, and then in the original language with the help of translations, and as I heard conversations mainly in Cardiganshire between Welsh people around me, between the farmers in the landscape which I regard very much as my landscape now — how else, what else would one be but influenced? The stories I heard the farmers tell were in Welsh, and they come into my poems in English. Also I'm very fond

of the seven syllable line, and I've got that from Dafydd ap Gwilym, and from others like him, though not necessarily consciously. And I don't use rhymes at the endings of lines, but at other places in the line, and that, too, is a very Welsh characteristic. I love using *cynghanedd*; I don't do this regularly as the Welsh-language poets do, but I let it happen and feel a private pleasure in it. It is something that puts an extra tremor or richness into the line. Also, occasionally the word that comes into a poem is a Welsh one, as in one poem where I use the word 'dwr' instead of water, because it was the right one to use on that occasion.[7]

The poem to which Gillian Clarke is alluding here is 'The Water-Diviner' which Tony Curtis suspects was at least in part indebted to, if it could not be entirely credited to, Seamus Heaney's 'The Diviner'.[8] But Clarke's 'The Water-Diviner' is significantly different from Heaney's poem. Whereas both poems hold the Diviner in some awe, Clarke equates the Diviner's skill with some kind of religious power. Here she introduces a comparison with prayer and the water is likened to a "voice" from the silent earth. Both poets appreciate the almost mystical quality, but Clarke stresses the efforts to draw the water which the Diviner has located. This somewhat different emphasis betrays the fact that Clarke is writing not as a spectator, but someone actively living in a rural area and needing water in a drought-bound summer. Heaney's poem closes with the movement of the stick in the Diviner's grasp, following the failure of members of the crowd who watch to get the same results themselves. Clarke's poem, on the other hand, closes with the gush of water: "dŵr...dŵr...dŵr". It is expressed appropriately in Welsh because the sound of the repetition of the Welsh-language word better conveys the movement of the water than the English-language 'water' would have done. Also the use of the Welsh language here reflects the way in which the mystical skills of the Diviner were better understood and appreciated in the older, Welsh-language, rural culture. The fact that Heaney invokes in his poem not prayer, but broadcast aerials as a metaphor for what he is witnessing, notwithstanding his appreciation of the mystical nature of what he is observing, betrays the way in which he is further removed than Gillian Clarke from the rural skills he is writing about. Of course, many of Clarke's poems are actually rooted in demanding, often exhausting, physical work: scything, harvesting, burning nettles, preparing mortar, syphoning water and shearing.

Many of Clarke's poems are also rooted in historical Welsh settings: 'Ystrad Fflûr'; 'Blaen Cwrt'; 'Clywedog'; 'Llŷr'; in her response to which she is typically Celtic. A sense of place is, of course, crucial to a sense of identity. As Nicholas Jacobs has pointed out: "a sense of identity is hard to envisage without the co-ordinates of existence afforded by the consciousness of a place in space and time."[9] And as he goes on to say: "it is through the interpenetration of tradition (time) and locality (space) that a community experiences its identity."[10] He recognises also that it is possible to have "an implicit sense of membership of a community without formal knowledge of the details of the sophisticated levels of the tradition", but that "it is when a loss of shared background becomes apparent that the need arises to formulate and to cherish a conscious idea of the tradition."[11]

The land — its traditions and geography — has always had a special place in Celtic cultures. And Irish poets, too, have drawn upon its physical beauty and above all its mythic significance.[12] Indeed, Seamus Heaney's insight into the Celtic appreciation of place applies to Wales as well as to Ireland. In 'The Sense of Place' (1977), Heaney describes two ways in which place is known and cherished: one "lived, illiterate and unconscious, the other learned, literate and conscious." The crux for Heaney is the symbolic nature of the landscape, "steeped in associations from the older culture" and the way that "the features of the landscape are a mode of communion with a something other than themselves, a something to which we ourselves still feel we might belong." Clarke is only too conscious of the way in which her native land has become two nations. In her poetry, she makes us aware, quite subtly, that discovering a cultural heritage and identity for Welsh people means reaching back to an older, pre-conquest Wales:

> And the mountains, in a head-collar
> Of flood, observe a desolation
> They'd grown used to before the coming
> Of the wall-makers. Language
> Crumbles to wind and bird-call.
>
> ('Clywedog')

'Fires on Llŷn', written in 1984, deals with the campaign of the 1970s and 1980s against English holiday homes in Wales which nationalists believed pushed up property prices so that local people could not afford to buy their own homes and turned communities into 'ghost villages' out of season. The poem hinges upon a momentary mistaken idea that the farm has been set alight. But it is only the sunlight in the distant windows. The Llŷn peninsula is where one feels physically and culturally close to Ireland and the poem gives voice to a fear that Wales might see a similar kind of violence to that which has occurred in Ireland. Yet there is also a strong awareness that Welsh culture has been destroyed by English hostility and indifference signified by the three English boys throwing stones. Subtly, the fact of the English boys throwing stones follows the poet's reverent observation that: "Any pebble or shell / might be the knuckle-bone / or vertebra of a saint."

The mistaken fires are seen through binoculars. Binoculars bring what is distant near and this really signifies what is happening in the entire poem. The poet has carved out for herself a specifically Welsh life in a rural part of Wales. Around this personal island of Welshness is an increasingly angry sea of protest: "See the hares run, / windows darken, / hear the sea's mumbled novenas." But the poem also suggests the multiplicity of linguistic, social and political factors which make up the political reality of Wales.

II

The importance of Clarke as a Welsh poet writing in the English language is rooted to a considerable degree in the way in which she thinks of herself as a Welsh person and as a woman. As she herself has explained:

> My loss of Welsh has been a very strong tension in my writing. But English is my mother tongue, and it is the tongue I was educated in. But being a woman and Welsh and therefore in two senses not wholly ready to count myself as one of the grown-ups, not easily able to feel I was permitted to be myself, to be a writer, an artist, I was a very late developer. Many women, particularly in Wales, are late developers as writers.[13]

Clarke's poetry highlights several aspects of what it means, and has traditionally meant, to be a woman, but one of the chief characteristics of the women in the poetry, such as Mamgu in 'Letter from a Far Country' and Marged in 'Marged', is their strength. In some poems this strength is an aspect of the way women cope, and have had to cope, with difficult lifestyles. 'Marged', for example, contrasts the lifestyle of the poet who now lives in the cottage with that of its former inhabitant. The poet comes over as better educated in the formal sense and mobile in the sociological sense with lamps to light the winter afternoons, whisky, books, a typewriter, a radio and a car. By contrast, the snapshot, as it were, from Marged's life — calling her single cow under the sycamore through the mud at the gate — is representative of her life's arduousness and austerity. But in other poems, the strength of women, the way in which they have had to learn to cope, is apparent in other aspects of their lives, two of which are explored in 'Letter from a Far Country'. Here women's lives are seen as being concerned traditionally with ordering and counting and with the problem of being cast in the rôle of the one who stays behind, waiting:

> It has always been a matter of lists.
> We have been counting,
> folding, measuring, making,
> tenderly laundering cloth
> ever since we have been women.
> ....
> The minstrel boy to the war has gone.
> But the girl stays. To mind things.
> She must keep. And wait. And pass time.

Both these rôles are fixed according to the argument of 'Letter from a Far Country' by a frame of reference which includes psychological, historical and socio-cultural perspectives. The eclectic nature of the poem itself shows, for example, how the rôle of women as the ones who wait is legitimatised by culture and custom on many levels including nursery rhymes, in which the boy with his belongings over his shoulder sets off to explore the world at the end of his lane, the ballads in which women wave men off to war, and the custom which accrues to men a right to the fields not enjoyed by the women who only enter the fields as a privilege.

Not surprisingly, the preoccupation with ordering, counting and making lists is seen as part of the historically determined rôle of women as the partner who looks after the house and the family. Clarke has herself described 'Letter from a Far Country' as an epic poem about housework:

> If the work of raising the generations is not epic, what is? If trenches, guns, blood are fit for poetry, as in the work of David Jones, why not kitchens, jam, nappies, birth! .... Why should the domestic not be a suitable subject for art?[14]

Some critics have argued that the poem succeeds "in spite of its domestic subject...".[15] Others have maintained that Clarke is the acceptable face of feminism: Curtis, for example, argues: "Her long poem 'Letter from a Far Country' succeeds as a feminist polemic where more directly aggressive voices have repelled those they would seek to change."[16] Both views ignore the anger in the poem. Hooker has taken a different line and argued that there is "anger and frustration", but because the poem is a love poem, the love "prevents rage".[17] However, we must be careful not to underestimate the anger directed, as Clarke says:

> against those who assumed I had all the time in the world and that all women have all the time in the world to do things simply because they live in a house and work in a house which is clearly a place where nothing goes on. It was also to do with the low valuation that is given to what women do.[18]

Early in the poem, Clarke declares: "The morning's all activity." The activity, its diversity and ceaselessness, is hammered home by the verbs: "I fill baskets..."; "I arrange the books..."; "I place your clean clothes..."; "I move in and out of the hive / all day, harvesting, ordering." The 'I' is strategically repeated, while the metaphors stun us into revaluing what a woman does:

> I draw the detritus of a family's
> loud life before me, a snow plough
> a road-sweeper with my cart of leaves.

Here not only is the tough nature of the work conveyed, but also, again, its ceaselessness: the snow plough and the cart have to return again and again.

Not only 'Letter from a Far Country', but many of her poems

are rooted, of course, in domestic situations. Indeed, some of the early poems, especially, begin like diary entries, such as: "Owain was ill today. In the night / He was delirious, shouting of lions"; "It was good tonight / To polish brass with you." Moreover, Clarke is particularly adept at mining the domestic for stunning images: from 'Shearing': "At tea-break we rest, the smells of wool / like wet Burberries going home from school"; in 'Castell y Bere': a lamb's head is portrayed as "clean as a toy, the beads / of its vertebrae picked smooth as hail maries"; in 'Snow on the Mountain' white slag tips are "like cones of sugar"; in 'Birth' the poet feels "satisfaction / Fall like a clean sheet around us." Perhaps one of the most striking examples is to be found in 'Journey', describing the way in which an old table is suddenly lit up by the car's headlamps:

> Once we saw an old table
> Standing square on the grass verge.
> Our lamps swept it clean, shook
> The crumbs into the hedge and left it.

'Letter from a Far Country' places the domestic rôle of women within a fresh and larger cultural context of selected, prioritised and socially-determined knowledge indicated by the way in which the narrator at the beginning of the poem sets about arranging books in alphabetical order within subjects. As the poem unfolds, the way in which women in the past have been the subject of this process of ordering, prioritising and classifying is signified by the graveyard of the parish where some of the narrator's ancestors are buried. The priority men have enjoyed over women is evident, even here, from the way their names and achievements are proclaimed on the stones, while the women are humbled by the simplicity with which their names are recorded:

> On the graves of my grandfathers
> the stones, in their lichens and mosses,
> record each one's importance.
> Diaconydd. Trysorydd.
> Pillars of their society.
> Three times at chapel on Sundays.
> They are in league with the moon
> but as silently stony
> as the simple names of their women.

Clarke, however, does not simply delineate the strength of women which has come from coping with traditional rôles and situations. She is interested in what all women share as a result of these. Thus women, through the rôles assigned them by biology and society, have had, traditionally, a special proximity to suffering and death. In 'Sheep's Skulls', a metaphor reminds us that in working-class, and especially mining communities, it was the task of women to lay out the bodies of the dead and this traditional practice is alluded to again in 'Taid's Funeral', where the dark incisions in the stalks of daisies are made by a woman's nail. In 'Suicide on Pentwyn Bridge', this closeness to suffering assumes a larger significance, becoming a basis upon which women are drawn together. The main focus here is upon the way in which the wife of the man who threw himself from the bridge into a long, lingering death, suffers alone. The communication barrier between herself and "the doctors who had no words, / no common supermarket women's talk" is opposed to the way in which the poet, as a woman, recognises the "long drawn-out falling in the brown / eyes of his wife week after week." .

Clarke's emphasis upon women as soul-mates has to be placed in the context of the historically determined, male-orientated cultural framework in which, and against which, Clarke, like all women in Wales, has to seek orientation and definition. The profound level upon which all women are soul-mates is particularly evident in 'Marged'. We have already said that the poem can be read literally, presenting an actual aspect of Marged's life which is also representative of her life as a whole. However, the "snapshot" from her life also carries other levels of meaning. The key details — cow, mud and sycamore — are traditional symbols of fertility: the cow is the mother Goddess; mud signifies earth fertilised by life-giving water and the fruit of the sycamore is milk-yielding. This level of meaning is dependent, of course, upon the reader being familiar with these traditional cultural and mythical associations. The selection and combination of three signifiers with the same connotation in a single event emphasises the female as the purveyor of life itself and creates the context in which the question is posed in the final line of the poem: "What else do we share, but being women?"

While the poem on a level of historical fact stresses the differences between the women as regards their lifestyles, the imagery suggests that they share inner qualities and awarenesses common to all women. While the historically-determined conditions of women's lives have changed on the surface, the fundamentals have remained unchanged. These fundamentals are part of a larger, collective consciousness that embraces women not just as individuals, but as female.

'Blodeuwedd', which is based upon a story in *The Mabinogion* in which Blodeuwedd is turned into an owl as a punishment for adultery, presents us with a sense of "sisterhood" rooted ostensibly in a sharing of domestic responsibilities:

> the comfortable sisterhood
> of women moving in kitchens
> among cups, cloths and running
> water while they talk,

The word "sisterhood" suggests a deeper bond between the women than is necessarily a result of what is described here, women moving and talking in kitchens. There is a sense of the atmosphere of a kitchen through the reference to cups, cloths and running water. But these selected features seem arbitrarily chosen, for there is much space between them. There are other, closer details that might have given a fuller picture of a kitchen's ambience. Like the three details we discussed from 'Marged' — the cow, mud, and sycamore — they seem to have been selected for what each sigifies rather than for the way they combine to create a visual scene. While each is representative of kitchens, each carries traditional symbolic associations which reinforce the profounder bond suggested by the word "sisterhood" than is fully justified on a literal level by what follows. Cups are traditionally representative of the "feminine principle", while running water is symbolically the water of life. So, symbolically, the poem points us towards a concept of "sisterhood" based upon the proximity of the feminine to the life source, as protector of life. In 'Sheila na Gig at Kilpeck', this collective female consciousness, as it were, is placed quite explicitly within the larger procreative context of nature:

> We share
> premonitions, are governed by moons

and novenas, sisters cooling our wrists
in the stump of a Celtic water stoop.

The association of the female and the moon is, of course, traditional, the moon signifying cyclic time, birth, death and resurrection and perpetual renewal. Clarke employs it even more
explicitly in 'The Hare' in the description of the relationship
that develops between the two female poets:

Then, that joke we shared, our phases of the moon.
'Sisterly lunacy' I said. You liked
the phrase. It became ours. Different
as earth and air, yet in one trace that week
we towed the calends like boats reining
the oceans of the world at the full moon.

It enters also into 'Letter from a Far Country' where Clarke
traces the bond that all women have shared, despite even the
differences between the generations, more fully than elsewhere:

We are hawks trained to return
to the lure from the circle's
far circumference. Children sing
that note that only we can hear.
The baby breaks the waters,
disorders the blood's tune, sets
each filament of the senses
wild. Its cry tugs at flesh, floods
its mother's milky fields.
Nightly in white moonlight I wake
from sleep one whole slow minute
before the hungry child
wondering what woke me.

The emphasis in Clarke's poetry upon reclaiming and developing modes of signification with a feminine rather than masculine
orientation is not surprising given the distinctive, masculine orientation of much Welsh cultural myth. Those lines are sand-
wiched between a description of the graves of forefathers "in
league with the moon" and an account of the inevitable inter-
ruption to her letter writing by the return of her children from
school. So, in addition to all its traditional associations, the
moon becomes a symbol of what imprisons women — as the
verb "trained" reinforces.

On one level, the poem delineates the bio-psychic bond between mother and child in fierce fashion: "breaks", "disorders", "sets...wild", "tugs", "floods". On another, through its symbolism, it places this bond in a broader context. The hawk, a symbol of strength and endurance, and an emblem of Amneti, the Great Mother, enjoys limited freedom like the mother who always has to return. The circle is emblematic of the feminine and maternal, suggesting the enclosing waters of the womb, wholeness, completion, fulfilment, but also closure and confinement.

A shared knowledge of pain, birth, suffering and death, is the crux of the bond that exists between mothers. In 'Scything', the poet as mother understands the despair of the warbler:

> There is stickiness on the blade.
> Yolk on my hands. Albumen and blood.
> Fragments of shell are baby-bones,
> the scythe a scalpel, bloodied and guilty
> with crushed feathers, mosses, the cut cords
> of the grass

But the symbolism of the poem, as here, lifts the bond to the level of myth in the post-structuralist sense. Cords suggest both the cut grass and severed umbilical cord. The symbolic meaning here is encapsulated in the symbol of the scythe itself: as an image associated with harvest. Traditionally, it is a symbol of time and death. But as an object in which the upright and the curved, and the functions of cutting and reaping, are combined, it is a symbol of the union of the male and the female.

Once again, we have seen how the symbolism in Clarke's work is both subtle and sophisticated. But the way in which Clarke's poetry articulates the complexities and tensions in the condition of being a woman and gives voice to the unexpressed emotions and experiences of women over the centuries is especially important for Welsh literature in English. As Deirdre Beddoe has pointed out, Welsh women have for too long been invisible in the context of the national image of Wales.[19] This, together with the way in which her Welshness is such an integral part of her sensibility and her poetry, helps to make Gillian Clarke one of our most important contemporary writers.

III

We have concentrated in this chapter upon Gillian Clarke because she is such a well-established and important poet who has done much to encourage other Welsh, and especially Welsh women, poets. But her concern with ancestry and identity is shared by other emergent poets, and not least by Sally Roberts Jones. *Relative Values* centralises Sally Roberts Jones' interest in the values which informed the lives of some of her ancestors and the way in which she stands in relation to those values. As such, it is an exciting development of a strong tendency in English-language, Welsh poetry to see relatives as "characters" and as "representative".[20] The entire collection is underpinned by the realisation that she is articulating what has gone largely unrecorded. As in Clarke's 'Cofiant', which should help us appreciate just how Welsh the concerns of Jones' book are, her memory and her family's memory acquire as much significance as what may be authenticated by records and epitaphs.

The poet in *Relative Values* feels indebted to distant ancestors, some of whom she cannot even name. What they have in common is that they were ordinary, uncelebrated people — "These, my people, are unrecorded" — and that many of them were 'Wrights' (craftspeople and makers) who in their own ways, like the poet, found a means of self-expression. Indeed, the language which she uses to describe herself as a poet —

> But in my hands
> I feel the shaping of words,
> The craft they gave.

— with a stress upon the "shaping of words" and upon poetry as a *craft* align her firmly with her non-literate ancestors:

> Their works remain elsewhere, in another script.
> Their history is the wheat, bowing to harvest,
> Ripe fruit on the strawberry canes,
> A row of carving, maker unknown,
> In a London East End chapel.

Some poems articulate the unsung, hard work of these relatives, many of whom were also, in their different ways, rebels.

The Cleaver who was sent to Botany Bay is remembered, ironically, because there is no romance about him and no "bushranger epic" celebrating him:

> He got on with the job; worked hard,
> Was paroled, found a place,
> Added penny to penny,
> Earned life.

The structure of these lines highlights the personal qualities that enabled him to adapt to the new world. The number of verbs packed so closely together — "He got on", "worked hard", "was paroled", "found", "added", "earned" — suggests not only the unrelenting effort, but the quiet, controlled determination which assured his success. The last two lines serve not only as an epitaph to this relative, but summarise the qualities which the poet believes he possessed and which she can accept and take from him: "He was not a remarkable man. / Only, it seems, a survivor."

However, the most important ancestor for Jones is her paternal great grandmother, Ellen Owen, who like Gillian Clarke's Mamgu is remembered for her strength of character, and was as much a rebel as the ancestor sent to Botany Bay. So much so, that she has become larger than life. Here, of course, Jones is writing within a cultural framework that places great importance on grandmothers. But the importance that Jones attaches to her is part of her concern as a Welsh woman writer to find her identity as a woman within a cultural framework which highlights the masculine. 'Ellen Owen' is concerned with the way in which the great grandmother has transcended time, and her own existence as a woman, in becoming a family legend:

> She's a myth as much as a woman.
> Grandfather's grandmother,
> Remembered by name, not by place.
> Ellen Owen.

The first line makes clear that this is not a poem about an ordinary woman of her times, while the second line, stressing how much time separates the poet from her paternal great grandmother, underlines the wonder that one who lived so far back in history can still exert such an influence in the present.

Ellen Owen was uncompromisingly forthright, forceful and independent. The physical strength — "Five husbands, a score of live children" — which enabled her to survive for longer than the official mortality rates for her day would suggest is matched by her mental acumen: "What she minded, she compassed." Our age is one that should be able to appreciate her: "Neither Mrs or Ms would express her" and she was "nobody's brood mare".

We are not given many biographical details of her, but we do have two snapshots, as it were, of the extremes of her life: in her drawing-room on the one hand, and toiling as a poor widow on the other. What is reinforced in these different views of her are her determination and her inner strength. In different ways on both occasions, she is in control and determinedly self-possessed: "she governed, sat prim"; "she toiled, / Foot-weary". It is a control that extends to her death at the age, especially significant for her day, of a hundred. The cliché that she was "a hundred years young" is relieved by the detail of how the first warning of death came to her: "Walking up from the market." Up until the very end she remains vigorous and independent: "For three weeks she held court." The last verse contrasts her self possession with the relatives and friends who seem at a loose end: the daughters busy themselves brewing tea, as if that is all they can do; her "respectable sons / Talked gravely of nothing"; while old friends can only think of their own deaths. The brisk efficiency of her death is symbolic of her attitude towards life: "Then, debts answered, sins pardoned, all done, / She turned over and slept."

Sally Roberts Jones' recreation in poetry of strong, female rôle models is important in Wales, as in Gillian Clarke's case, because of the way in which the national image of the country has tended to honour only its men. This is the key to the poem about the execution of Margaret, Countess of Salisbury. The crux of the poem is the opposition of the reality of Margaret — "the grey-haired old woman" — and the element of farce in her being chased around the execution block with the final triumph which she scores in her refusal to consent to her own "murder". The execution is deprived of the dignity and sombre ritual which legitimises it: the executioner is exposed as an "embarrassed killer", his axe becomes a "bloodied steel" and he is robbed of the status and dignity of his office as the words "waving" and "futile rage" signify. Even though she is eventually caught and executed, the truth of Margaret's protest remains, undermining the epithet "justified" in the description of the King's throne.

While Ellen Owen, Margaret and the Cleaver who was sent to Botany Bay, were rebels in their different ways some of the other ancestors were more conformist. But the poems concerned with them still question and probe the relativity of values. This concern with the relativity of values is part and parcel of the way in which many writers at the margins quarrel not only with the larger forces of hegemony that threaten their cultural origins, but with those myths within their own cultures that threaten to constrain them.

Determination and courage and the ability to get on with it in a stiff-upper-lip kind of way are what the poet discovers — or thinks she discovers — and admires in 'Alfred Cleaver Grew'. The opening line of the poem about him is the only one which contains his actual words and in many ways they summarise the man as a whole: " 'I should be there', he said." The values informing this declaration are those of his age: a sense of duty combined with deep-seated courage. In the following lines, the key words are "he thought he saw":

> ...he thought he saw
> A duty that would compel him to enlist,
> Not knowing how time and misery would make
> Such acts seem the lesser follies of the mad.

Immediately, the poem focuses upon how values are themselves relative. The bold, self-confident view expressed in the words actually spoken by Alfred Cleaver Grew in the first line of the poem is opposed to the poem's reported account of what he actually said later about the campaign:

> he spoke of the flies, only flies,
> And heat, and the stinking dust.
> He was, I suppose, disillusioned.

The last line here is not only a brilliant piece of understatement, but suggests that the old man kept on top of his "disillusionment", remained, as it were, in control.

While this is admired, there is also concern over the way in which the old man was never able to leave behind the reticence of his upbringing:

> A man
> Whose actions were certain, whose motives
> Were always unknown.

The poem closes on a disquieting note as the way in which his actions seem "certain" to outsiders is opposed to the motives that are kept so deeply hidden. The actions are *too* certain; the motives *too* hidden.

Uncle Emrys is similarly a worrying combination of courage and silent strength. Again, it is the inflexibility — "He waited alone"; "And he stood" — together with the way in which he is divorced from what now surrounds him and makes him appear "the fearful, the alien shape" that is disturbing:

> (Like something out of Boys Own; the intrepid explorer
> Faced with the need for miracles —
> But nothing so simple —)

As Jones demonstrates in earlier poems such as 'Dic Siôn Dafydd Returns to the Valley', she has no time for people or communities content to live in illusions of the past. 'Palm Sunday /Sul y Blodau' concerns the custom in South Wales of putting flowers on family graves. The opening verse takes a detached, wry look at the country bus making its way from one chapel graveyard to another: "You might call it the dead run." The perspective of this first verse is important, with the stress placed on the custom, signified by the bus, over and above the individuals who participate. The women — who are only mentioned after the flowers — are merely "cargo". The description of the bus trundling along the high road signifies the cumbrous way this custom has managed to survive into the twentieth century. Only in the second verse does the poet-narrator emerge fully as a participant and an individual as she confesses to her involvement in the ritual with a degree of surprise: "I too" and, later, "And I too will descend."

The sense of detachment and the slightly deprecating humour of the first line of the poem, which in some ways undercuts this particular custom, are the products of the realism which underpins the poem as a whole. There is an air of pleasant unreality about the Palm Sunday ritual which the poet never allows to develop:

> I ride among beauty, these delicate trumpets of April.
> It is almost a pastoral: sunlight, white clouds on blue oceans,
> New buds on the branches, lambs leaping —
> The wind's knife at their throat in the sunshine.

The poem lulls the reader, as the flowers delude the poet, into a false sense of security before the rude awakening of "The wind's knife at their throat...". The device of setting up a response and then undermining it is used again later in the poem. The end of the third verse describes the poet's work that day in restoring order:

> Will harvest the weeds, wash the mud stains
> Away from the stone, place new holders
> In leaking memorial urns.

The verbs here — "harvest", "wash...away", "place" — suggest a triumph over the forces of decay represented by the "weeds", "mudstains" and the "leaking memorial urns". But the opening of the fourth verse takes a different view of these events and the balance changes in favour of the latter. The confidence of establishing order, other than momentarily, has disappeared:

> Earth under my nails, feet half frozen,
> I wedge fallen jars with the chippings
> Against the wind's malice; ...

The restoration of the graves is, of course, symbolic of a larger interest in preserving ancestral lines and continuities:

> It seems
> A curious, silent beginning
> Beneath the sharp rain.

The way in which the homeward bus journey is described is significantly different from the delineation of the "dead run" in the first verse. The individual now seems in control: "Later, on the bus, I ride homeward...". Here the poet-narrator is using the bus and not appearing as the prisoner of the bus. The "patchwork of meetings, conversations" may be taken literally as a description of the patchy inter-relationships between "annual strangers" on the bus, but it also signifies the way in which the past, unavailable as a coherent body of knowledge, is at best fragmentary. Indeed, the way in which the past is available to us is an important motif in the collection. As Jones says thinking about her own ancestors in 'The Wrights': "A few scraps of gossip / Decorate the plain lines of their book." In 'Not a Tolpuddle Martyr', the evidence is equally insubstantial:

> Only the nuance of legend admitting his cause,
> Suggesting that more than a prank or a hooligan hour
> Ignited that haystack.

Relative Values, as the pun in the title suggests, relies heavily upon information transmitted orally from one generation to the next. These familial legends and myths service a deep-rooted need within individuals to define themselves in relation to their ancestral lines and provide a wealth of accumulated historical experience which many poets writing at the margins are currently mining in their work.

IV

The third poet with whom we are concerned in this chapter has been chosen not only because he is a significant emergent voice, but because he is representative of English-language, Welsh poets who have returned to Wales to reclaim an ancestry. Like a number of Welsh poets writing in English, Oliver Reynolds tried to learn Welsh as an adult. At first, it might seem rather exploitive for such a poet to publish a body of poems in English with Welsh-language titles; an attempt to jump on a bandwagon without taking on board seriously the issues involving the Welsh language in Wales. However, as far as the third section of *Skevington's Daughter* is concerned — nineteen poems with Welsh-language titles — this is not the case.

Given that Reynolds is a Welsh poet writing in English, it is not surprising that guilt soon raises its head in these poems:

> Each has his reason to be here
> Speaking through declenched teeth:

> I'd thought it time to stop
> Welshing on the language
> And learn about roots,
> If only etymological ones.

The kind of wit, punning on "declenched" and "Welsh", displayed here is typical of these poems. The wit, however, is not a carapace, but an integral part of the poetry; a way of coming to terms with, understanding and articulating a sense of estrangement in a country that is linguistically, politically and socially divided.

Appropriately, this section of *Skevington's Daughter* begins with a poem which subtly suggest how Wales has been exploited for minerals for England — "We're in mined territory" — and the way in which many Welsh people, consciously or unconsciously, have denied their roots and concludes with a poem, 'Dimai', (Welsh for half-penny), in which the coin is a symbol, like the ticket in R.S. Thomas' 'A Welshman at St. James' Park', of the divided nation. The poem can be read upon two levels: either as a poem about the new decimal coin, the linguistic idiosyncrasy of calling it a "ha'penny" and the case for its continued circulation, or as a poem about the Welsh language. Two positions are assumed as regards the coin: the detractors claim it is used less and less and should be retained, if at all, only for nostalgia's sake, while those who actually use it in their everyday life and work argue for its retention. The poem is particularly successful because of the way in which the metaphor for the Welsh language is sustained throughout. It is riddled with language which has to do largely with finance and currency: "devalued"; "accounted"; "stability"; "coinage"; "hoard". The metaphor, though, is more than a structuring device. The poem urges us to redefine what we regard as valuable and shifts the focus of our attention to the value of non-material things. The selection of the half-penny as a metaphor is especially appropriate because the Welsh language, as a minority language, is like the smallest coin, most likely to be taken for granted or ignored, and most likely to be discarded. The phrase "devalued by large forces" suggests the way in which small, Welsh-speaking areas have found it difficult to cope with, say, the large influences of English colonialism, centralisation, the attraction of places outside of Wales, and the Anglo-American dominated mass media. But the poem makes the crucial point that each use that is made of the Welsh language, however small, helps to keep it alive and the poem closes on an optimistic note by acknowledging how supporters of the Welsh language are learning to "disregard other coinage".

The particular stance that we adopt, as individuals, to the Welsh language is deemed important in other poems too. In 'Ifori' ('Ivory') the poet steps out, as it were, from behind the metaphor:

> The choice is ours — as with language:
> We opt for retreat or ambush,
> Aiming to snooker or impale.

Yet the total impact of the poem is dependent, once again, upon metaphor. Thus, the ivory is said to be viewed from two possible angles: as something raw on a live elephant where "tusked, / It can ram or pierce'; or as something dead, taken out of its natural context, and used to fashion piano keys or snooker balls. The language and the personification used to delineate the latter point of view — the ivory "smiles evenly from pianos" and on snooker tables "kisses and cushions" — smacks of compromise.

The use of humour and metaphor to make statements about the Welsh language may be indicative of the political climate in Wales, where active campaigns for the Welsh language have tended to make more obvious political poetry appear too much like naked political statement. Yet in this section of *Skevington's Daughter*, where the poet is concerned not only to discover a Welsh heritage, but to understand and articulate what has happened in Wales and to unravel a web of complex political and social forces, humour and wit become effective tools with which to work. As is suggested in 'Halen', which concerns the poet's adult learner classes in Welsh, only in childhood do teachers, say, have easy answers, and thesis and antithesis neatly oppose each other:

> Pent now within these four walls,
> The world deflates to blackboard size.
> Shrunk to neat opposites, it falls
> Prey to white chalk and whiter lies.

'Nodiad' may, on a cursory reading, seem a glib piece written to amuse. For D.J.s in Broadcasting House to note that "*Ll* and *ch* in Welsh resemble / *Xl* and *r* in Xhosa" will not help them much! But the poem is actually about the way in which the B.B.C.'s seeming indifference to minority cultures is symptomatic of a larger institutionalised and hence legitimatised indifference. The title of the poem, 'Nodiad', meaning 'Note' is, at least in translation, ambiguous: both a brief note and *note bene*.

The title of the poem, 'Pobl y Cwm', means 'People of the Valley'. The fact that the title is in Welsh indicates that the "people" are in many ways the indigenous population of the valley with roots in the mining community going back to the industrialisation of the area or are people who migrated there to work and put down roots. Here, Reynolds' concern with the present, like that of the poets from Northern Ireland and the North of England whom we have already discussed, is entwined with history and his sense of history, too, is highly politicised. Now that the valley has been exploited the mines have been closed. In their place is a factory making designer underclothes. The humour of the poet's response — "We read our future / In the bottom of a D-cup" — is appropriate because the factories like the mines are taking advantage of the valley and its people. The brand labels appeal to the middle class, carry a reputation made outside of Wales, and have nothing to do with the valley as such. The poem suggests that the factories will offer little to the valley in the long term as the glib response of the last verse indicates: as a lover, the poet trying to undo a bra claims his fingers "Busy themselves with nothing less / Than the plight of Welsh industry". The humour here stands in sharp and telling contrast to the vivid delineation of the valley after the mines have closed:

> We fossick through slurry
> And our thin sodden days:
> Life on the canal bed
> After the plug's been pulled.

The first two lines suggest not only anger, but the frustration of struggling. The bed of the drained canal with the repetition of the 's' sound suggesting the sordid sludge becomes a metaphor for the malaise and quality of life in the valleys now. The days are indeed thin, both materially and spiritually, while the last two lines suggest exasperation that all this has been done by forces outside of, and beyond the control of, the area.

There is an attempt in 'Bechgyn Bando Margam, 1800-1859', as in Gillian Clarke's work, and Seamus Heaney's, to look back to a more holistic time, a period when within a particular locality there was a sense of genuine, communal identity. As Reynolds explains in a note to the poem, Bando is a game, remotely like hockey, which was very popular in Wales in the nineteenth century. The focus of the poem is not upon the game and its rules so much as the involvement of the players in making the ball and the sticks themselves. Behind this involvement are skills which have themselves disappeared; a skill, for example, which is reflected in the ability to whittle wood into the shape of the ball. The period during which the game was played is seen as a kind of cultural hiatus — "Their heyday was decades long" — and this idea is suggested again when the men are said to have been "set free on the heights of summer". The communal and the private are opposed; pit and furnace set against "common land". This is a time when the communal dominates: not only is the land on which they play "common land", but there is a sense of sharing: they will have made their own sticks, and "pitched the posts with the other team". All this underpins the sense of pride implicit in the conclusion of the poem: "They will have stood out clearly / Under the sky's primary blue / In their red and white." Like Seamus Heaney's poems about his forefathers, this one is concerned to urge the reader to reconsider and revalue the past, the communality, the sense of sharing, the pride: "Their heyday was decades long / And is now forgotten". Significantly, the colours are the Welsh national colours: "They were red and white / Like others later."

'Bechgyn Bando Margam, 1800-1859' becomes a poem about nationhood, about the national pride that existed when there was a sense of community and, most significantly of all, as suggested by the involvement for the preparations of the game, when the people had control over their lives. In the poem this sense of control is achieved away from the pit and the furnace. On one level, we have here the working-class man's desire to find his true self outside of the work which denies and erodes it. But within the larger context of the way in which the pits and

the furnaces were an imposition upon Wales, a form of imperialism, "snatches of Arcady / Won from shifts", it becomes
doubly significant. The pits and the steelworks point to an English culture, but the Welsh game, signifying the life of the community away from these, recalls an older, Welsh-speaking
Wales so that, once again, the Welsh title of the poem proves
significant.

In Part One, we highlighted how the cultural framework in
which many Welsh poets work has proved problematic because
of the claims of rural Wales upon definitions of Welshness.
Oliver Reynolds' work has a particular bearing upon this issue.
Unlike Gillian Clarke, with agrarian roots on both sides of her
family, Reynolds cannot return vicariously with ease to the
older, rural Wales. Some of his writing betrays the influence of
R.S. Thomas at his most disturbed and churlish. Like R.S.
Thomas, Reynolds sees little romantic in the Welsh countryside
which for him is bleak and essentially static. 'Cefn Gwlad' complains: "Always like this"; "Nothing to do". As in R.S. Thomas'
case, Reynolds' quarrel is with the parochialism and the limited
imaginative horizons. The poem stresses the rain: in the first
verse we have the relentless "falling rain"; in the second verse
"the image fixed / Many years back" of "Land, sky and rain";
in the third verse the "rain sealing" the horizons. This sense of
being confined within limited horizons is embodied in the
structure of the poem itself. 'Cefn Gwlad' opens and closes with
verses which have the same opening line — "Always like this"
— though by the time it is repeated it has become burdened by
an extra weight of meaning. And the second and third lines of
the poem — "The standing field" and "The climbing cloud" —
are also the ones which close it. R.S. Thomas' influence also
seems to raise its head in the rather churlish opening of 'Poeth
ac Oer': "Season of small gains / In a land of small victories."
But the reliance of R.S. Thomas and others upon rural Wales is
challenged in 'Daearyddiaeth'.

'Daearyddiaeth' (in English, 'Geography') acknowledges the
rural tradition in Welsh poetry written in the English language,
but also recognises that, since much of Wales is urban, this
tradition of rural poetry does not hold much meaning for the
majority of the population. The poem opens by addressing the
inhabitants of an older, rural Wales for whom the land was

their whole life. Three of the five lines of the first verse begin: "The land was..." and the verse itself presents a holistic society where the land "was always worked", "was in your heart", "was underfoot". Here the land provides the people with their livelihood and is also an emotional reality. In the second verse, the poem acknowledges that, although farming methods are changing, the land is still worked. But the difference is that the emotional significance of the land for many Welsh people has become divorced from the practical, everyday life and is preserved in songs sung at rugby stadiums and in poetry which for its inspiration looks back to rural Wales. The consequence of this is that love and the land have become one. The second half of the poem presents a two-pronged attack upon the way in which the rural has become synonymous with Welsh culture. The city has been generally ignored in Welsh poetry in English and there is little to which lovers in urban contexts can relate. As is typical of Reynolds' poetry, humour is used to make a serious point. In traditional Welsh-language poetry he claims: "While streams grew feminine / Desire and greening joined." Urban born poets, though, are advised to "exchange Arcady / For the brick of Cardiff." Reminding us of the humorous way that love was treated by metaphysical poets such as John Donne, and thereby leaving himself open to similar charges of flippancy and chauvinism, this suburban poet suggests how the urban love metaphor might be developed:

> Fingers that divagate
> Along the vertebrae
> Assume Sanquahar Street,
> Sesquipedalian
> Way to the timber yards.

Yet even here when he is tending towards glibness, Reynolds is still attentive to language. The fingers of the lover assume a wandering course signified by the snake-like cumbrous word, "sesquipedalian", which reflects what it describes, and the repetition of the 'S' sound which again suggests the snakelike wandering of both the fingers and the spine they are exploring. Just as Sanquahar Street strays, as it were, to the timber yards, the wandering fingers find their goal, with Reynolds indulging in word-play based on the lumberjack's warning cry of achievement: "Timber!"

It is difficult for an author to write about love and sex without his/her love and sex seeming to be more important, intense or fulfilling than anybody else's as it is difficult to insist upon one's own individuality without seeming egocentric and arrogant. On both accounts, Reynolds' humour is a safeguard in circumstances in which love, sex, and individuality is both an escape from, and an answer to, the burden of a divided cultural heritage. This is apparent not only from 'Daearyddiaeth', which tries to acknowledge urban love experiences in the face of a poetic tradition which has ignored them, but 'Pobl y Cwm', which we discussed earlier, where the "fingers fighting Gordius" in the final verse is the poet's personal individual stand within a context of socio-economic change that cares nothing for the individual. These contexts, together with the exciting and conscientious use of language, enable the poet to get away with three incidents of wandering hands along a feminine spine in a single section of *Skevington's Daughter*!

In both 'Pobl y Cwm' and 'Asgwrn Cefn y Beic' the last lines remind us of the Welsh cultural dilemma in a humorous way. But, in each case, the last line only reminds us of what was raised in more subtle ways earlier in the poem. This is especially true of 'Asgwrn Cefn y Beic' which is threaded with an ambiguity of language, one level of meaning of which keeps the Welsh dilemma always before us. The use of language is as subtle and as sophisticated as that of 'Dimai' which we discussed earlier. The poem suggests the conquest of Wales by the Marcher Lords, while keeping to the fore the immediate situation — the seduction of the female cyclist by her male companion. Thus, it begins with the male making tentative, first moves towards the girl's spine, still sticky from the perspiration of cycling, but employs the verb, "foraging", which is more commonly used of armies in their rummaging. The physical sensation of the insouciant fingers along the spine are described in the third verse:

> Giving in taut waves, folded flesh
> Hummocks above the knuckling bones'
> Smoothed and stubborn crenellation.

On one level, we have here a description of the girl's back as it responds to the kneading fingers. But the language develops the military associations of the word "foraging" in the first verse. "Crenellations" is an apt description of the vertebrae down a young, and presumably, slender back. But, literally, it can mean "battlements". Hummocks are ridges or hillocks to be found, especially, in marsh land while "Castling" reinforces the suggestion of military fortifications, but also refers to the manoeuvre in chess which is a key part of many defensive and attacking strategies. The full significance of this latter meaning becomes clear in the following line where the girl is said to have been "mated":

Castling, he skims the long hollow,
Mated, grinning, she shuts the book.
His fingers, Marcher Lords, push south.

This account of seduction ends on a note of complicity: "grinning, she shuts the book". The book is *The Third Policeman* in which cyclists, it is claimed, become to varying degrees the bikes they ride. The suggestion here is that the anglicisation of Wales was rooted in a process of seduction and complicity since many Welshmen literally sided with the English lords and in post-conquest Wales sought places at the English Court for themselves and an English education for their children.

While the use of Welsh language titles for English language poems in the third section of *Skevington's Daughter* may appear opportunist, the poems embody a profound and serious commitment to some of the issues of identity and culture in Wales. An understanding of the commitment involves us in an appreciation of Reynolds' skill and sophistication as a poet.

The three poets whom we have discussed in this chapter seem very different. But in each case we find a concern with culture, ancestry and identity, a highly politicised sense of history and an awareness of the present as historically determined. An interpretation of myth in the post-structuralist sense as a mode of signification rather than in the traditional sense helps us understand how Gillian Clarke and Sally Roberts Jones as Welsh women write from a quarrel with the historically-determined, male-orientated cultural framework of Wales and seek to emphasise myths with an alternative feminine signification. Oliver Reynolds' work provides an interesting contrast to that of Sally

Roberts Jones because he tries to reclaim a generalised national, political and social ancestry through the Welsh language, while Jones is concerned to reclaim a wider ancestry through a particular familial ancestry. Oliver Reynolds' poetry also offers an engagement with those issues around language, politics and nationalism in Wales highlighted in Part One. The next two chapters take up the concerns highlighted in Part One with reference to the work of poets from the North of England who again offer an interesting contrast to each other.

CHAPTER FIVE

THEM & UZ: TONY HARRISON'S ELOQUENCE

Why must I be father and son,
hating and loving across years?
I want to take my own hand,
and in a still place in the wind,
be what I have become.
    John Woods ('Looking Both Ways Before Crossing')

A personal father, and that is one clear issue. But a father is more than a person, he's in fact a society, the thing you grow up into. For us, perhaps, that is the way to put it. We've been moved and grown into a different society. We keep the relationship, but we don't take over the work. We have, you might say, a personal father, but no social father.
    Raymond Williams (*Border Country*)

I

The sonnet sequence, *from 'The School of Eloquence ' and other Poems* (1978), expanded in *Continuous* (1981), has been described by Anthony Thwaite as Tony Harrison's "central achievement".[1] Much of the energy of individual sonnets stems from conflict: for example, between a working-class schoolboy and a middle-class teacher; between an unbookish father and a scholarly son; between a working-class man and the society that makes him feel an "oaf".

Harrison is the working-class lad lifted by talent and education out of his working-class background, out of the legacy of male, working-class relationships, guilty at having somehow betrayed his roots, yet unable, even if he wanted, to deny his intellectual gifts. In this sense there is a strong affinity between Harrison and the poet Roy Fuller who, too, was lifted by education out of his Northern, working-class background. Like Harrison, Fuller at times felt guilty over the way he had divorced himself from his roots. As in Harrison's case, the rift between himself and his past was exacerbated by the loss of his native accent, but he was not haunted by his background to the extent which Harrison seems to be in *from 'The School of Eloquence.'*

As we highlighted in Part One, much of what we have to say of working-class poets in the North of England applies to poets of similar origins from other parts of England, Wales, Ireland and Scotland. But the North of England does have a more problematic relationship to the conventional parameters of cultural power than that of many other areas.

In many ways, the literary antecedents of Harrison's sonnets are the working-class novels of the 1950s by writers such as Sillitoe, Storey, Braine and Barstow, whose heroes such as Joe Lampton, move from their working-class origins into a new middle-class identity harassed by private guilt. In 'Them & [Uz] I and II', Harrison displays not only guilt, but lingering resentment over the attempts to force him to deny his native dialect and his past. 'Them & [Uz] I' draws a parallel between Demosthenes, who filled his mouth with pebbles to cure his stammer, and the poet himself, "mouth all stuffed with glottals", trying to rid himself of the Leeds' working-class idiom that brought him ridicule in school from the poetry teacher:

> 4 words only of *mi 'art aches* and... 'Mine's broken,
> you barbarian, T.W.!' *He* was nicely spoken.
> 'Can't have our glorious heritage done to death!'

A lot has been condensed into these few lines. The first line structurally reflects the way in which the teacher interrupted Harrison and the speed of the interjection underlines the sharpness of the teacher's wit as he takes up the word "heart". The way in which the boy is humiliated by this is underlined in the contrast between the insult and the poet's own caustically loaded comment: "*He* was nicely spoken." But the changing of the phrase "my heart" into "mi 'art" by dropping the "h" is pertinent in another respect for the poem is literally about *mi art* from the poet's point of view, an art which is rooted in both high and working-class cultures. 'Them & [Uz]' acknowledges that aesthetic judgements transpose distinctions of class into distinctions of taste. In calling Harrison, the schoolboy, by his initials, "T.W.", and by labelling him a barbarian, the teacher uses the possession of cultural capital to legitimise the domination of his class over the working-class from which Harrison has sprung. By acquiring education and/or cultural capital, as it were, himself, Harrison is able to move into a higher class not as Tony, but Anthony Harrison: 'Anthony' is sophisticated, but distant, formal and rather cold; 'Tony' is warm and friendly. There is also the suggestion in this poem that working-class and upper-class views of art are opposing perspectives. Harrison may move into a class higher than the working class, but that does not mean he automatically trades one view of art for another. He will never be able to become fully middle-class except in the most external sense of the label. When Harrison discovered that Keats was a Cockney and that Wordsworth wrote in dialect and not the received register, he found precedents for writing legitimately in his own dialect and for taking a different view of art from that of the upper class which understands the possession of art, cultural capital, as signifying the possession of eloquence and power from which others are excluded.

from 'The School of Eloquence' is rooted in a debate between the upper-class and the popular views of aesthetics. The poetic form chosen, the sonnet, is a formal and sophisticated verse form and as such signifies one side of the debate: a view which equates art with good taste, excludes recognition of the practical or ethical functions of art and is more concerned with intertextual than with mimetic modes of reference. However, the sequence pays more than a fleeting regard to the popular view of art which values continuity between art and life. The debate comes to a head in the argument between father and son over the epitaph for the mother's tombstone:

> Come on, it's not as if we're wanting verse.
> It's not as if we're wanting a whole sonnet!
> .....
> You're supposed to be the bright boy at description
> and you can't tell them what the fuck to put!

In the poem, 'A Good Read', Harrison admits: "I've come

round to your position on 'the Arts' / but put it down in poems, that's the bind."

Many of Harrison's poems derive their force and pathos from the rediscovery of his native dialect, education having provided him with the confidence "to tell the Receivers where to go". (The pun here is typical of Harrison's ingenuity.) The fact that Harrison came from a working-class background and acquired middle-class English largely at grammar school provides him with some original perspectives on language. He uses language in more innovative and exciting ways than he might have done had he become accustomed from an earlier age, and at home, with middle-class English. In particular, the fact that he stands between cultures, as it were, has enabled him to look afresh at both his native dialect and his more formally acquired English and exploit the poetic potential of both in tandem as it were. This provides his poetry with a special kind of vitality, especially as far as its imagery is concerned. For example, in 'The Rhubarbarians': "Those glottals glugged like poured pop"; in 'Me Tarzan': "His bodiless head that's poking out's / like partriarchal Cissy-bleeding-ro's"; in 'Divisions I': "Teenage dolewallah piss-up, then tattoos / Brown Ale and boys' bravado numbs their fright." In his poetry, there is an emergent and subtle interweaving of sound and meaning rooted in a reverence for language understandable in a writer who has escaped by his own powers of articulation from a class handicapped by its limited language. Often the interweaving of sound is part of an intricate blending of formal English and dialect as in 'Me Tarzan': "Off laikin', then to t'fish 'oil all the boys, / off tartin', off to t'flicks but on, on, on."

The interplay of sounds in the poetry is frequently concomitant with the assimilation and development of different layers of meaning. In 'Blocks' the single line, "Blocks with Letters. Lettered block of stone", juxtaposes the alphabet blocks with which the poet learned to read and ultimately write; his mother's tombstone; and the block between himself and his relatives.

The development of metaphor through word-play and ambiguity gives many of the poems the coherence which Harrison first achieved in *The Loiners*. Hence, 'Marked with D.' highlights two aspects of his father's life — that he was a baker and 'kept down' socially by class barriers — through the association of a baker's mark on a loaf with the dunce's cap marked with a 'D'.

The first line of the poem associates the baker's ovens with the cremation ovens, and his father's flesh with the dough he used to put into his ovens. The dough/his flesh is "chilled", a word which not only suggests death, but prepares us for the later mention of his "cold tongue". The tongue is "cold" in the sense of being dead, but cold also because his father was inarticulate. Hence, in turn we are prepared for the later description in the sonnet of "the tongue that weighed like lead". This in itself stands in contrast to the way in which he always called his wife 'Florrie', a name which has more warmth and love in it than 'Florence' and carries more respect than 'Flo'.

Figurative and literal meanings again coalesce in the description of the father's cataracts "ablaze" with Heaven. His eyes are imagined as "ablaze" in the figurative, religious sense, but also "ablaze" in the literal sense of burning within the cremation ovens. The ambiguity is sustained in the ruminations about his lack of articulation in the last part of the poem. Harrison ponders how his father "hungered for release from mortal speech". "Release" here suggests both his desire to be articulate and a desire for release from life into death after his own wife's death. The poet himself doubts that there is an afterlife and once again the imagery is rooted in the fact that his father was a baker: "I get it all from Earth my daily bread."

Throughout 'Marked with D.' word-play and ambiguity are not simply adornments but integral parts of the poem. So when we learn that Harrison's father is "the baker's man that no one will see rise", the word "rise" suggests the way that his father was not allowed to improve his social status because of the class system while connoting the yeast his father used to make his bread rise. His father was always made to feel "like some dull oaf". The sound of the last word cunningly reminds us of the "loaf" with which his father was associated even before we meet the word when the rhyme scheme is completed later.

Appreciating the echoes and cross-references within single poems in the sequence helps us to understand their coherence and subtle structuring as well as the breadth of meaning within each poem. But while the sonnets may be read and enjoyed as individual poems, the more we become aware of Harrison's ear for the interplay of sounds between formal English and dialect, and of the interweaving of echoes and cross-references, the more the complexity and breadth of *from 'The School of Eloquence'* impress themselves upon us. Often a sequence of lines, or even single lines, are riddled with echoes of, and cross-references to, other poems in the sequence, in order to sustain a larger body of meaning.

In 'Cremation', for example, the poet describes how his father, when he was in company, would keep behind his tongue the phlegm which tended to build up at the back of his throat and how, only when alone, in front of his own fire at home, would he hawk "his cold gobful at the brightest flame." Not surprisingly, a number of words here anticipate 'Marked with D'. The phrase, "brightest flame", carrying obvious religious connotations, anticipates the flame in that poem into which his tongue bursts in the oven but never did, in a metaphorical sense, throughout his life. The fact that the "gobful" is "cold" prefigures the "cold tongue" of 'Marked with D'. It is cold because it has been kept in his mouth for some time, and cold in so far as it suggests the lost opportunity of someone who has only been able to work in lowly manual positions all his life.

The image of his father hawking his gobful is repeated in 'Currants II', in the poet's memory of his father getting up early for his shift at the bakery, while the word "hawk" itself is used in 'Them & [Uz] I' in Harrison's account of his attempts to rid himself of his native dialect: "my mouth all stuffed with glottals, great / lumps to hawk up and spit out...". "Gob" is slang for mouth and also a northern term for a worked-out section of a mine, an ambiguity that Harrison exploits in 'Working' to suggest that his father also is worked-out. In fact, throughout the sequence there are references to mouths, to being inarticulate, and to the desire, and the struggle, to become articulate. Thus, Harrison with his mouth stuffed full of glottals is compared in 'Them & [Uz] I' to Demosthenes, the stutterer, "gob full of pebbles outshouting seas". While "gob" here is echoed in 'Cremation' and 'Working', Demosthenes, as a stammerer, echoes the way in which in 'Heredity' and 'Self Justification' Harrison attributes his skill as a poet to an uncle who was a stammerer.

In 'Self Justification', punning on the meaning of 'justification' in printing, Harrison applies the word to himself: "I stammered my first poetry / that made me seem a cissy to the lads." The guilt over identity here is typical of that which underpins the whole sequence: the word 'cissy' setting off a further echo with 'Me Tarzan', which describes his early anxieties over being a poet within a working-class culture.

If we trace the cross-referencing between the various poems closely, we come to appreciate the depth of this guilt. 'An Old Score', for example, is one of many of the sonnets that turn the spotlight upon it: "Capless, conscious of the cold patch on my head / where my father's genes have made me almost bald." Here the speed with which the poem moves in two lines from the poet's consciousness of himself to his consciousness of his father impresses on us the extent of the anxiety. And the way this line echoes another poem illuminates one of the causes of it. In 'Working', his father's increasing baldness is coterminous with a general decline in his father's health and physical well-being. The effect of this cross-referencing is to expose the poet's anger over the way in which his father was exhausted by a lifetime of manual work. But as the sequence of sonnets probe the anxiety, a rôle emerges with growing confidence for Harrison as a poet.

It is commensurate with the concern over articulacy and inarticulacy that the rôle that Harrison assumes, as Young has pointed out, is as spokesperson for "the inarticulate, mass of people who have been exploited throughout history without being able to protest or even cry out".[2] This becomes one of the key motifs of *from 'The School of Eloquence'* which declares:

Three cheers for mute ingloriousness!

Articulation is the tongue-tied's fighting.
In the silence round all poetry we quote
Tidd the Cato Street conspirator who wrote:

Sir, I Ham a very Bad Hand at Righting.

The fact that Harrison sees himself as tongue-tied in 'Self Justification' — the "aggro" of his teenage peers he confesses there is "what keeps my would-be mobile tongue still tied" — and feels his own father's anguish over his verbal inadequacy makes the cause both personal and political. It is important to realise that in the sequence his father exists both as an individual and as a representative of a tongue-tied class. He is placed in context with others from history, the famous such as Tidd and the unknown such as the paperhanger in 'Remains'.

In 'Remains' the thousands who "traipse round Wordsworth's Lakeland shrine / imbibing bardic background" are opposed to the poet who alone notices the one line, written with humility by the paperhanger, "so discrete / it's never trespassed" on "the poet's' aura". Wordsworth is, of course, part of the canon of English poetry to which nearly every schoolchild is introduced and the language — "traipse", "shrine", "bardic background" — implies that the visitors who come to the Lake District do so only to visit a vestige of the past. But as we know from 'Them & [Uz] I', Wordsworth meant more than this to Harrison, as one of the poets who helped him to establish himself in his own identity as a poet of working-class origins. In this identity the paperhanger's line has a special significance for him because both have their origins in the class of forgotten, powerless and inarticulate people. Again there is a cross-reference here with 'The Earthen Lot' where the pun suggests the lot of different classes on earth as well as the mortality of which we are all, irrespective of class, victims. In 'The Earthen Lot', it is axiomatic that those who are articulate also have power and the influence to buy sheltered graves for themselves, while the inarticulate and the powerless are assigned graves nearer the erosion of the sea, a position which itself, ironically, reflects their status while they were alive.

There is, though, another dimension to this rôle of spokesperson for the inarticulate which, again, emerges from the cross-referencing between poems. Harrison shares Seamus Heaney's concern with the way in which he was made to feel inferior because of his dialect. In 'John Bull's Other Island' (1977) Heaney, like Harrison, feels himself torn betweeen "words of the heart and hearth — language and the learned, public, socially acceptable language of school and salon". In 'Singing School', he casts himself in a similar rôle to that in which Harrison found himself in the Leeds Grammar School:

> Those hobnailed boots from beyond the mountain

THEM AND UZ: TONY HARRISON'S ELOQUENCE

Were walking, by God, all over the fine
Lawns of elocution.

But Harrison's anger, inherited, like his bald crown, from his father, is more specifically targeted. In 'Cremation' when his father finally spits his "gobful" into the fire we are told that he is "too practised, too contemptuous to miss". Some of Harrison's own accusations are as "contemptuous" and aimed in the same direction as his father's spit. In 'Turns', Harrison declares: "I'm opening my trap / to brusk the class that broke him...."

This contemptuousness is part of a much larger world-view that has its origins in the working class North of England as a poem, outside *from 'The School of Eloquence*,' and entitled, appropriately, 'Facing North', suggests. In this poem, Harrison realises that he will always "face North", both literally at his desk and metaphorically in the stance assumed in his poetry. In other words, the North has been "internalised".

As a poet, struggling with issues of identity, Harrison fluctuates between anxieties and a sense of security that he feels the North and his working-class past provides. In 'Facing North', the former are signified by the images and sensations created over and around his desk by the swirling of the paper lantern that hangs from his light bulb:

> images of planets hurled,
> still glowing, off their courses, and a state
> where there's no gravity to hold the world.

The picture here is of chaos: "off their courses" suggests also the colloquial expression for madness, "off their heads". And the idea of madness is picked up by the poet in the next line: "I have to hold on when I think such things / and weather out these feelings...". What helps him to hold on are some of the values of the subculture in which he grew up:

> where elbow grease,
> deep thought, long practice and much sweat
> gave me some inkling of an inner peace...

All this must not be confused with a sentimental nostalgia. Despite the affinity Harrison feels with the North, anger and despair inspire what are among some of his most innovative uses of language. Removed from his native environment by education, he is also distanced from it, as *The Loiners* confirms, by having lived and worked abroad. All this makes him conspicuously aware of the austerity and harshness of Northern cities such as Durham. The first stanza of the poem, 'Durham', suggests an unwelcoming environment and climate. However, this environment (represented by fading graffiti on crumbling stone) and climate (represented by constant drizzle and fog) are metaphors for the soul of the place which Harrison also tries to encapsulate in the harsh, almost spat, syllables:

> A butcher dumps a sodden sack
> of sheep pelts off his bloodied back,
> then hangs the morning's killings out,
> cup-cum-muzzle on each snout.

These lines are overly conscientious, almost straining for effect, but they are successful because of the way in which they are contextualised within the poem as a whole, preceding a panoramic view of the city which takes in antennae, the spires and visiting choirs — the guide book city — and anticipating the later imagery.

In communicating the harsh soul, these later images are as pertinent as they are innovative. The city, for example, is seen as a "dog / chasing its own cropped tail", which takes up the sense of being encircled suggested in the second stanza (where "lifers, rapists, thieves, ant-size / circle and circle at their exercise" almost beneath the prison helicopters) while the "cropped tail" signifies the sense of thwarted development that underpins the poem's view of the city. The hail is envisaged as "teeth spit from a skull", an image that takes up the undercurrent of violence first suggested in the graffiti, the butcher's killings and the handcuffed prisoner in a black sedan, a car synonymous, of course, with gang violence in America.

The external view that Harrison is able to take of the North, of working-class dialect and of middle-class English extends to his view of society and of himself as a poet. The fact that he saw his father as part of a crushed and disappearing class seems to make him sympathetic to the plight of animals that are on the point of extinction. The title of the poem, 'Killing Times', is typically ambiguous suggesting the time which he has to "kill" in waiting for his plane at the airport, but also the character of the milieu in which he is living with its preoccupation with killing. The fact that he sees himself reflected in the exhibition case signifies the way in which the poet as a figure is becoming increasingly redundant in a mass media and technological age.

Yet Harrison is rarely pessimistic. As he says in 't'Ark' — the dialect of the title is especially significant linking the Leeds working class with all crushed peoples: "Silence and poetry have their own reserves." We have to note that "reserves" is double-edged suggesting both reticence and an untapped resource. The *Peppered Moth* in 'Dark Times' is a symbol of the effects of industrialisation and the way that society and people have adapted to it. But the prospect that the moth may one day appear white over Leeds is an indicator of Harrison's faith in the future.

II

Within the class warfare, the conflict between them and 'Uz', in the sonnets there is an even more personal and poignant purpose. The sequence is informed by the poet's attempt to try to rediscover his father and to reach posthumously a sympathetic appreciation of him. As the ambivalent title of 'Long Distance' indicates, the poet and his father have not felt close to each other and have been communicating "long distance", as it were, for some time. Ironically, fathers spend much energy worrying about establishing a relationship with their children, as B.S. Johnson summarises in 'Occupation: Father':

> Undoggedly I interest myself
> in his uninteresting concerns
> grow backward to him,
> more than hoping to find
> a forward interest for myself.

But the son as an adult spends as much energy "growing backward" in order to find the father which he never had the maturity or experience to appreciate. Moreover, in patriarchal, working-class cultures, such as that in which Harrison grew up, the relationship between father and son is especially significant. As David Lusted has pointed out:

Fathers, like mothers, can care ... but, of course, they must always
retain their power...

More than the caring rôle, however, father figures are most im-
portantly teachers. They share the knowledge that advanced age or
superior experience of the world brings, especially to sons. Here
the male points to the knowledge, not just of his own biography
remember, but also from that sense of national biography. He
passes on a legacy of male relations and male society. Legacy,
inheritance, knowledge, power. This is the sense that childhood,
like nation, is male. Like father, like son.[3]

It is the widowing of his father, that inspires the poet to try to
understand and articulate the distance that has come between
them as if his mother was the buffer that enabled them to
preserve their distances. On more than one occasion, the reason
for their mutual hostility dawns on the poet amidst angry self-
reproach as in 'Book Ends I': "what's still between's / not the
thirty or so years, but books, books, books." Additional tensions
arise from the ambiguity of the poet's individual, as opposed to
family, roots. In 'Me Tarzan', when Harrison, the schoolboy, is
called by the 'Twelfth Street Rag' from his scholarly attic, he
yells back in his Leeds dialect: "*Ah bloody can't ah've gorra Latin
Prose.*" He is contemptuous of his studies partly because he is
bored and would like to go with the others, but also because of
the working-class cultural attitudes of his peers which dictate it
is unfashionable to be studious and even more so to be a poet
which makes him "seem a cissy to the lads".

The analysis of the photograph in 'Background Material' encapsulates this salient theme of the sonnet sequence. Typically,
the title is ambiguous. On one level, it refers to the unvarnished
verism of the background against which the photograph has
been taken, his father's favourite pub. On another level, it refers
to the particular social and cultural milieu from which the poet
as well as his father came. The pub has been demolished, signifying the way in which this social and cultural past has virtually
disappeared. But most significant of all, the photograph is
marred, from a professional point of view, by the reflection of
himself in his father's eye. This reflection symbolises the way in
which a father always has expectations of a son and the bond
which always must exist, for good or ill, between them. But on
the photograph of his mother, the reflection appears as a sha-

dow, signifying that it was she who first introduced him to the words which came between him and his father. The movement in the poem is from a perspective which sees the two photographs as separate to realisation that they share a frame, both literally and metaphorically.

The pursuit of an understanding of the "frame" which all three share impels the reconstruction of the quarrels between Harrison and his father in *from 'The School of Eloquence.'* Even the smarting, emotional welts left on the son by the occasionally sharp tongue of a "clumsy talker" are remembered in an attempt to probe the subtleties of what it was that came between them.

The sonnets try to establish a communication between father and son that never existed when they were together as a family and was not easy even after his mother's death. 'Long Distance' encapsulates his father's misery and loneliness as a widower: it emphasises the way in which the family home, now empty, has become unbearable and the way in which when the father says he is missing his wife's cooking, he really means he is missing the company of a shared meal. The phone-call which gives rise to the poem and which is allowed to "take its dismal course" imposes an almost impossible emotional burden upon the son. The interplay in the poem of narrative voice and the father's whining dialect suggests the emotional tension between father and son who now find themselves yoked together by new obligations and dependencies.

In 'Illuminations I', poet and father come closer together as they do also in 'Still'. 'Illuminations I' is based upon a family incident on Blackpool's Central Pier after the Second World War in which the poet is criticised by his father for putting too much money in the slot machines. As the ambiguous title (referring to both the Blackpool Illuminations and intellectual enlightenment) suggests, the poem moves to an understanding, and acceptance, of the father's point of view. The final line is addressed to his father himself, again with one of Harrison's sharp puns: "The penny dropped in time! Wish you were here!" The much used colloquial expression for seeing the point links the last line with the father's complaint. The phrase "in time" suggests not only that it has taken a long time for the father's point of view to be appreciated by his son, but that his son is lucky to still have had time in his own life to achieve at least a posthumous reconciliation. This, of course, heightens the pathos of the wish, so glibly placed at the end of postcard messages, but having a rare sincerity and profundity here. Of course, understanding his father means that the son must take account, perhaps for the first time, of how he must have appeared to him, a key feature of 'Illuminations II' where, recalling how he lectured his parents on science, he realises that his father must have thought him a bore.

Several of the occasions upon which Harrison remembers as a young boy receiving a smarting, verbal swipe from his father are ostensibly "male situations". He remembers in 'Currants I', for example, an occasion upon which he was taken by his father to the bakery. The invitation is an attempt to cement, if not establish, a bond of "male solidarity" between them. He is taken to be "wi' t'men". The daydream of undressed girls in which he indulges in a way reinforces the bond for it presents us with men-without-women indulging in men's thoughts of women. However, the poet, as a young boy, insults his father not only by refusing to sample the currants because his father's sweat has fallen into them, but by rejecting the "male bond" between them. Sweat implies hard, 'masculine' graft and it is regarded as somewhat 'unmasculine' to be fussy about a little sweat among the ingredients. Significantly, next Sunday he is told he can stay "'ome wi' yer mother!".

An occasion is remembered in 'Still' when the poet was humiliated in the barber's shop by his father's insistence, contrary to his own wishes, that the barber put Brilliantine on his hair. Traditionally, the barber's shop, before unisex hair-stylist salons, was a male preserve, affording an opportunity for men to meet as men-without-women. The boy's decision not to have his hair plastered with oil because it causes him to leave greasy finger prints over his school work is also an attempt to assert himself as a male in a male context. The father's contradiction is all the more hurtful because he does not know, and it is implied would not care if he did know, that indirectly it is affecting the boy's work.

The Irish poet, Paul Muldoon, also remembers occasions in similar 'male' contexts when the bond between father and son as two males was important and when the son felt the need to establish himself in his own right within the masculine line, as it were. 'My father and I and Billy Two Rivers' from *Quoof* (1983) concerns the male camaraderie built around wrestling and the popularity of Billy Two Rivers, a Mohawk Canadian wrestler, whose matches are watched on television in the local barber's shop. Everyone in the shop believes that the whole thing is a "sham". Two Rivers might be defeated one week, but the next he is victorious. Similarly, masculine rituals are known to be no more than shams yet it is regarded as important to go along with them.

Since Harrison belongs to a family where masculine pursuits and rituals have had an important place, it is not surprising that he should feel the need to justify his rôle as a poet in the light of his ancestry. He discovers a few precedents. His closest affinity is with an uncle who was a stammerer and who became a printer. But that ink-staining, messy and, in those days, quite heavy work, even though it required both skill and aesthetic judgement, has more credibility than being a poet.

Notwithstanding this, there is also an attempt to justify his quarrel with the masculine ethic. It is exposed as a mask which hides and inhibits a more "feminine sensibility" which is part of all of us. Hence, the skinheads in 'Divisions I' who undress in the baths strip off more than their clothes. They strip down to tattoos of 'MOTHER' which reveal an emotional dependency which they otherwise cover up both literally and metaphorically. Ironically, what they now reveal not only belies their "macho sensibilty", but has a lot to do with poetry, the antithesis of this ethic.

Harrison's identity crisis is in some ways contextualised in the figure of the skinhead. As Dick Hebdige has argued, skinheads are themselves a product of a working-class, cultural identity crisis: they look back not to a real, but to a mythologised working-class community "with its classic focal concerns, its acute sense of territory, its tough exteriors, its dour 'machismo'...".[4] In this sense, there is a parallel between British working-class, Welsh and Irish communities for each tends to look back through discontinuities to an idealised past.

Several of the sonnets address Harrison's father's confusion of identity. In 'Next Door IV' he complains: "smelling curry in a pop shop. Seems all daft."; thereby identifying a tangible social change: the presence of black people in traditionally white, working-class areas. But this only signifies other tangible changes underpinning the estrangement of father and son: the breakdown of the extended, working-class family, the substitution of private for communal space, and the embourgeoisment and the erosion of traditional, working-class values. The sequence is riddled with references that suggest Harrison's father is the last in a traditional familial line and the last representative of a particular way of life: in 'Cremation' he has the last coal fire in the smokeless zone; in 'Book Ends I' father and son eat the "last apple pie" and in 'Next Door II' the father is the last to keep the small, front garden tidy. He also sees himself as the last white inhabitant and he is the last to make an effort to clear the winter snow and ice. In 'Next Door IV', it is said that the "old lot" cannot come back.

Eventually, the concern with the past in the sonnets opens out into a wider perspective beyond his father and beyond his quarrel with, and need to define himself against, his father's working-class, very male-orientated culture. 'Lines to my Grandfathers' is typically ambiguous in so far as "lines" refer to the poet's penned lines, addressed to his grandfather and great-grandfather, but also the ancestral lines from them down through his own father to himself. The poem is important because it lifts him out of a rather repressive concern with his own parents and enables him to place his own life in a broader context. As he comments: "My present is propped open by their past...".

V began when Harrison tended his father's grave during the miners' strike of 1984 and recalled his father telling him, when he was a boy, that beneath the graveyard was a worked-out mine. Not only does the graveyard become a symbol for a worked-out class and generation, his father's generation, but also a symbol for Harrison's sense of his ancestry. The grave where his father and mother are buried is also where his father's mother and father are buried. It has one more place in it — possibly his own! This causes Harrison, as he admits in the opening of the poem, to think about how, as a poet, he belongs with those who are buried there: butcher, publican, baker. The graveyard also overlooks the city of Leeds with views of the grammar school and the university, the institutions which provided Harrison with the education that took him away from his ancestral background. Indeed, the range of language within the graveyard — including epitaphs in Latin, snatches of hymns and prayers, extracts from the Bible and graffiti, mainly in the form of blunt four letter words such as "cunt, piss, shit and mostly fuck" — reflects the class divisions and the inequalities within society. The 'V' sprayed on the obelisks signify for Harrison "all the versuses of life", "the unending violence of *US* and *THEM*". While the sense of conflict is underpinned by the miners' strike of 1984, which is the epitome, or to use Harrison's own word the "personification", of the deep-rooted oppositions within society, the poem tries to put these "versuses" into a larger perspective drawing up virtually a catalogue of the different levels of conflict:

Hindu	Sikh
Soul	Body
Heart	Mind
East	West
Male	Female

The poem also hinges upon the incidental meaning of the word "united" sprayed by vandals on his father's grave and meant to stand for Leeds United. To the fore is Harrison's guilt over his rôle as a poet and the struggle of the poem is not only to try to understand the motives behind the vandalism, but to unite the occupation of being a poet with his familial and class ancestry.

The skinhead's voice that suddenly intrudes into the poem, engaging the poet in debate, is the poet's alter ego. When he sprays his name on the grave, the skinhead sprays 'Harrison'. The poet and the skinhead are the two poles of Harrison's being — signified by the twilight at the end of the poem. The skinhead is what the working-class boy of *from 'The School of Eloquence,'* who bored with his study would rather have played with his peers in the street or have gone to the cinema, might have grown into. This boy is the grown-up his parents might have understood better in some senses than the boy who became a poet and who would have been in some ways truer to his working-class origins.

The fact that the skinhead is a projection of an aspect of Harrison's psyche is obvious not only from the way that he sprays his name as 'Harrison', but from the way much of what he says about the poet could not have been known to a stranger. The skinhead voices some of the poet's deepest guilts, anxieties and reservations. The poet is asked why he cannot speak the language of his mother, a barbed remark aimed at Harrison's rejection of his native Leeds dialect, and he is reminded of how she regarded his poetry, especially *The Loiners*, as obscene. But no sooner does the skinhead alter ego make Harrison aware of the familial rifts, then Harrison turns to his rôle as spokesperson for the inarticulate. The poet declares to the skinhead that the reason he wants to write *V* is to give those like him a hearing and to give what they do a larger significance. In this dialogue, Harrison ponders for the first time in his work how the inarticulate would regard his attempts to articulate in poetry on their behalf. In doing so, he begins to explore and acknowledge how, as an educated and in some ways now middle-class poet, he has grown apart from these people. Hence, when the poet mentions "aspirations" they are thrown back into his face. The unemployed "dole-wallahs" of Leeds have as "much scope to aspire" as "coal / aspires to be chucked on t'fucking fire". He comes to realise that the graffiti expresses the resentment of the unemployed over the fact that all the people in the graveyards had jobs and often the one occupation that they held all their lives. Not only did they have jobs, but crafts which gave each of them a sense of dignity and self-esteem when alive (notwithstanding how they may have been used and abused and never allowed to rise by the class system). In contrast, the skinhead football supporters of Leeds will probably only be able to have on their graves that they were unemployed. Just how much this strikes a chord with Harrison is underlined by the skinhead's shame that they may meet their mothers again, unable to boast of having made anything better of themselves. For, as we suggested above, Harrison himself was shamed and haunted by his mother's disgust over his first book *The Loiners*.

Also involved here is the contrast between Harrison's poetry and the raw, crude anger of the skinheads. In defence of his seeming passivity, Harrison, the poet, recalls a time when he, too, out of anger and frustration protested by setting off a fire extinguisher and had the epithet 'vandal' shouted after him.

Here poet and skinhead become momentarily united, ironically in view of the angry contempt expressed toward the vandals in the early part of *V*, emphasising how the skinhead's anger has an affinity with that which informs much of Harrison's other poetry.

The way in which the skinhead begins speaking in *V* with a four-letter swear word, 'cunt', recalls the way that Harrison opens the second sonnet of 'Them & [Uz]': "So right, yer buggers, then!". But while the anger that the skinhead displays is similar to that in Harrison's 'Them & [Uz]', Harrison is able to put it to more sophisticated use and expression:

> We'll occupy
> your lousy leasehold Poetry.
>
> I chewed up Littererchewer and spat the bones
> into the lap of dozing Daniel Jones.

The first two lines here suggest the way that poetry — as cultural capital — is associated with the property-owning classes. "Lousy" is both working-class slang and a description of being "louse infested" and as such continues the squatting association of the word "occupy" in the previous line. "Chewed up" and "spat", conveying the kind of protest we would expect from the skinhead in *V*, betray Harrison's interest in words and images associated with the mouth, while the word "littererchewer" displays contempt for the association of literature with institutionalised culture and for the way that the recitation of literature, especially poetry, in many schools became a kind of verbal mouthwash.

In the early part of the poem, *V*, Harrison notes that one of the Vs looks like a red tick, one of the ticks that the skinhead may never have received for his work. Although Harrison eventually did well enough to attend university, he, too, knew what it was not to receive due recognition and credit in the school system. When the skinhead threatens him not to use Greek, he is underlining the rift that education has placed between them: Greek epitomising not only the educational level of attainment that Harrison has reached, but signifying education — a classical education — as cultural capital.

What really hurts Harrison, the poet, however, is the skinhead's denunciation of him as a "wanker". The word is an assualt upon his working-class manhood and is recalled towards the end of *V* when Harrison's wife, naked, enters their bedroom to come to his bed. The impact of the insult upon a man of working-class origins is underlined by the way in which Harrison refers to his wife here as "my woman" in traditional working-class terms. But in order to appreciate why the word "wanker" has such an impact upon Harrison in *V* we have to understand how it rekindles for him the way in which writing poetry, as Harrison admits in 'Self Justification', made him feel a "cissy" in the eyes of his working-class peers and the way in which his long hair and his poetry made him seem, as he says in 'An Old Score', effeminate to his father:

> When it touched my ears
> he dubbed me Paganinny and it hurt.
> I did then, and do now, choke back my tears —
>
> *Wi' 'air like that you ought to wear a skirt!*

Of course, releasing the fire extinguisher was a spontaneous act of angry protest. It was the kind of behaviour which he eventually realised that he had to reject. And although at first the graffitied grave enraged him, he knows that he has to move beyond this type of instinctual reaction to something more rational and exploratory. But *V* does acknowledge what may be lost in this process, a kind of integrity and raw energy he tries to embody in the poem itself.

At the end of *V*, it is another accidental meaning carried by the graffiti — "united" — that offers a resolution of the conflict between the poet and the skinhead. As is made clear earlier in the poem, the word reminds Harrison of his father's love for his wife, Florrie, and his belief that they would be "united" again in an afterlife. Not sure at first whether this seizing upon accidental significance is but an excuse for avoiding cleaning off the graffiti, he decides to leave the word on the gravestone where it remains to inspire the belief at the end of the poem that the endless conflicts within society may be transcended by "love and sleep's oblivions". This provides the *raison d'être* for the poet to give himself to art and hence to the poetic imagination which transcends conflict.

The word "united" in this poem also emphasizes the way that, posthumously as it were, father and son have come together. There is the same sympathy for his father here that we saw developing throughout *from 'The School of Eloquence.'* He understands now his father's anxiety over the way in which the world in which he lived and spent most of his married life seemed to be receding from him. In this respect, *V* takes up ideas from the earlier sonnets and expands upon the confusion that his father felt as his neighbourhood became, for example, more and more multicultural. It is not that his father was necessarily racist, but that the past against which his life made some kind of sense and in which his roots lay was now disappearing.

The fact that the particular meanings of the word "united" which confirm the poet in his rôle come from his father's life and ambitions reinforces the extent to which son and father have come closer together. *V* closes with beef, beer, bread, the three necessities which his ancestors provided, to which Harrison now feels "poetry" can be added. At the end of *V*, Harrison has come to understand why the skinheads have vandalised the graveyard with aerosol cans; has resolved the tension between his occupation as poet and those of his forefathers; settled the conflict within himself between the two poles of his being; and come closer to his parents. In other words, he has "settled" his place within his ancestral line.

III

The way in which *'from The School of Eloquence'* works out a complicated relationship between father and son is echoed in the work of several other contemporary poets who, like Harrison, have familial origins in a patriarchal, working-class milieu. Although it never inspired an entire sequence, as in Harrison's case, Seamus Heaney's relationship with his father, for example, was similarly problematic.

Like Harrison, although not developed to the same extent, the Irish poet finds himself shackled with his father as a poetic subject:

> I was a nuisance, tripping, falling,
> Yapping always. But today

It is my father who keeps stumbling
Behind me, and will not go away.

Indeed, despite the differences, there are a number of parallels
between the two poets in this respect. Like Harrison, Heaney is
haunted by guilt. As Morrison has pointed out, he felt that "to
express himself freely, through literature, was in effect to betray
the values of the tribe".[5] But, also, as in Harrison's case, the
problem is not just one of guilt; it is of establishing one's place
in the ancestral line, or as Morrison expresses it: "how having
been educated out of them, to keep faith with one's family and
tribe". In an interview with John Haffenden, Heaney admitted:

there is indeed some part of me that is entirely unimpressed by the
activity, that doesn't dislike it, but it's the generations, I suppose,
of rural ancestors not illiterate, but not literary.[6]

Paul Muldoon's *Quoof* (1983) also opens with a poem in which
he, like Heaney in 'Digging', remembers his father engaged in
manual activity. In Muldoon's case, his father is gathering
mushrooms. Like Heaney, Muldoon looks back through his
father, as it were, to a rural inheritance, although for Muldoon it
is a less intense inheritance than for Heaney. There are simi-
larities between the two poems: in Heaney's case twenty years
separates the event from the memory; in Muldoon's case almost
as many — fifteen — years have passed. Like Heaney's father,
Muldoon's parent is totally embroiled in his physical activity.
The rhythm of the work is stressed in both poems.

Like Heaney, Muldoon, in reuniting with his father, is vicariously orientating himself towards an older, rural Ireland. His
father is "one of those ancient warriors / before the rising tide."
But to return imaginatively to an older, rural Ireland does not
mean leaving the country that is still trying to understand and
resolve its history, as the magic-mushroom induced nightmare
which concludes the poem, where he articulates the views of
dirty protester and hunger-striker, suggests:

lie down with us now and wrap
yourself in the soiled grey blanket of Irish rain
that will, one day, bleach itself white.
Lie down with us and wait.

THEM AND UZ: TONY HARRISON'S ELOQUENCE

The early poems of *Quoof* are about Muldoon's need, as in the case of Heaney and Harrison, to define himself in relation to his father and to come to terms with the masculinity that he has inherited from, and shares with, his father. As in Heaney's case, there is the awareness that his father will never quite go away:

> He was no longer my father
> but I was still his son
> I would get to grips with that cold paradox,
> the remote figure in his Sunday best
> who was buried the next day.

In all three cases, the conventional, literary solutions of crises in familial identity — rejection of formative influences or retreat into the past — are rejected for they do not square easily with lived experience. Each lives in a world where meaning, sense and value have to be searched and worked for. The father is representative: of the bounded space that bonds them to their own lives, their history and identity.

CHAPTER SIX

A POLITICS OF BEING:
THE POETRY OF DOUGLAS DUNN

I stand, if you like, with the ghosts of my grandfathers. It's an antagonism towards the way in which people think about nature as well as about society... a politics of life, or of being, rather than a politics of politics. — Douglas Dunn

Although Douglas Dunn is often referred to as Hull's "other poet", his origins are Scottish. While his father was born in Halifax, his father's parents were Scots. In fact, he admitted: "I'm a Scotsman with self-conscious Scottish interests, though I don't live in Scotland, and I don't know the majority of the people in the Scottish-literary scene."[1] However, Dunn is included in this study not because he is Scottish, but because he was one of the first poets to explore the way in which identities centred on objective notions of class have become increasingly uncertain. On his mother's side, his grandfather was the "co-operative baker in the town of Hamilton; a very kirkly man, an old left Socialist of considerable conviction."[2] Interestingly, in the interview with John Haffenden, he stresses his male ancestors, endorsing the importance of male ancestry in working-class culture.

His own origins are in "a very old village and parish" to the west of Glasgow: "an ordinary, respectable, working-class background." It was "a messily semi-rural kind" of environment quite unlike Terry Street, where he lived for two years. The latter, however, provided him with an opportunity to reflect upon the nature of the working class as it then presented itself to him in contrast to the older working class in which he had his own origins. But it does mean that while Harrison writes from within the Northern working class, Dunn writes from outside it.

Indeed, it is the exploratory nature of *Terry Street* which Dunn has himself stressed and which is responsible for what Anthony Thwaite has described as the "slow, circumstantial rumina-tion"[3] of the collection:

> I mean, the deliberation that went into the writing of the poems could be greatly overrated, and at certain times I have felt tempted to rewrite these poems and introduce motives I didn't have when I wrote them. I think I wrote *Terry Street* unself-consciously and what they add up to, if anything, is a matter for the reader to decide. I certainly didn't organize any particular thesis.[4]

Of course, we cannot ignore the fact that Dunn's origins are *Scottish* working class. Although Dunn has been aligned with the North-East more than with Scotland — Anthony Thwaite's survey of British Poetry from 1960 to 1984 devotes a chapter to Harrison and Dunn in tandem, as it were — the concern with identity in his work can be traced back to his Scottish roots. He complains himself of how "Irish writers, and certainly English writers, tend to be much more secure in their identities than Scottish writers...". Yet he advises us that we approach his poetry not as of Scottish, but of non-English origins: "I don't have an English accent and I don't think like an Englishman."[5] What he is recommending is the approach which we suggested earlier might profitably be taken to Welsh writing in English.

Douglas Dunn has never left behind his concern, in one way or another, with his origins, but the nature of that concern has changed radically between *Terry Street* (1969), *St. Kilda's Parliament* (1981), *Elegies* (1985) and his recent work. *St. Kilda's Parliament* has a breadth of perspective which takes in the range and variety of people who sit in Saint Kilda's Parliament from Robert Tannehill and John Wilson, a poet and teacher, to slandered Presbyterians and a boy admired by Sir Walter Scott. In many ways, it is a more accomplished and intellectual work than *Terry Street*. But the shift of critical attention and acclaim to his later work has tended to relegate *Terry Street* to a more inferior status in relation to Dunn's other work than it deserves.

In our discussion of the way in which the tripartite theme of culture, ancestry and identity has been as much to the fore in the work of poets of working-class as of Celtic origins *Terry Street* deserves pride of place. It was never his intention, as some reviewers originally believed, to write "scenes from working-class life". Dunn himself has described *Terry Street* as "a fictionalized version of what was around me...", written because he felt a stranger in the street and town in which he lived.[6] Dunn is concerned with working-class culture in the way in which culture has come to mean 'lifestyle' rather than, in the strict dictionary definition of the word, "a state of intellectual attainment". Dunn's perspective is different from that of the working-class characters about whom he writes in his poetry; he does not see them as they see themselves or as they view each other. Dunn's own origins, as we said, are different from theirs, in an older, working-class culture. This, together with the way he has left behind his own working-class origins in some (but by no means all) respects, gives the poetry a critical and rather distanced perspective.

We have already discussed Tony Harrison's awareness of how working-class communities of the kind in which he grew up had been eroded, and of how his father seemed to have been among the last representatives of a particular working-class milieu. But Dunn, impelled by his own rather different working-class ancestry, has a much more sharply focused and even more detailed understanding of the nature of this change. In the late 1950s and the 1960s, working-class life changed radically as patterns of consumption changed. But the new patterns of consumption evolved within, before they transcended, class boundaries. Dunn is concerned with the new working class, a working class with shorter working weeks, with more leisure and with more money to spend. Their leisure was, of course, commodified and cinemas, bingo halls, discos, magazines replaced home-grown, popular leisure forms and rituals. Money was spent on conspicuous symbols of status — especially clothes — and new signs around which new identities were constructed. Dunn's accounts of the new working classes focus upon "the way they had accepted all the paraphernalia of pop culture, and the extent to which a large part of their lives had actually been formed by that...". Without sufficient money to become truly mobile — outward and upward — they had enough money to be, as it were, at least 'upwardly immobile'. This point is made towards the end of 'The Clothes Pit': "But they have clothes, bright enough to show they dream / Of places other than this, an inarticulate paradise, / Eating exotic fowl in sunshine with courteous boys." Like Harrison and Heaney, as one who has become articulate despite his origins in an inarticulate class, he is aware of how his peers in that class did not and do not enjoy the same powers of expression. This is one of the themes that underpin 'The Clothes Pit'. Commodity fetishism is a mode of self-expression for those denied other means of articulation.

Throughout the poem, there are implicit and explicit comparisons between this new, consumer working class, the older, working class of Dunn's ancestry and the new, consumer middle class:

> In the culture of clothes and little philosophies,
> They only have clothes. They do not need to be seen
> Carrying a copy of *International Times*,
>
> Or the Liverpool Poets, ...

In one respect, the working classes come off better in this poem than the middle classes in so far as they do not have the intellectual dishonesty of the latter. The middle classes wear ideas as the working classes wear clothes. But the effect of this comparison is to underline how the working classes have failed to develop intellectually: "In the culture of clothes and little philosophies / They only have clothes." The new working class is seen as consisting of totally passive consumers, and what they purchase, is ephemeral: "impermanent coats" and "the litter of pop rhetoric". Of course, their new money gives them a degree of control and of freedom — "they mix up colours" and have nights out in pubs — but eventually all this is unsuccessful: they end up "fat and unlovely" and come home "supported and kissed" but "bad-tempered".

In some ways 'The Patricians' is the companion poem to 'The Clothes Pit'. In a consumer-orientated, *now* society the elderly have no real place. They have no value as workers and no interest themselves in keeping up with fashion. Unlike the young, they have the breadth of experience to be aware of what is merely ephemeral. The lack of interest shown towards them by others within the poem, in contrast to the poet's interest in them, signifies the way in which they have been discarded by a society which lives for today and sees people in the end as expendable.

The "small backyards" in which they are able to preserve their dignity by hanging out their old-fashioned clothes in private become a symbol of the way in which the old throughout the poem try to hang on to their dignity. The scarves which constantly muffle their throats epitomise the way in which they muffle themselves protectively against a younger, more assertive, outside world — signified by the chatty women in the laundrette — in trying to preserve their own solitary peace. By referring to them as the "patricians" of their streets, the poet invests them with a dignity and status they do not possess in reality. In the last verse, not only do they die alone, but they lie undiscovered. The middle-aged children who have deserted them, getting on with their own lives in the new estates, signify much deeper social changes and attitudes such as the way in which the members of the new, consumer working class take advantage of new opportunities and become increasingly mobile only at the expense of their own families and their origins.

Throughout *Terry Street*, we feel the presence, hardly ever made really explicit, of Dunn's own Scottish, working-class origins functioning as a benchmark against which the Humberside working class is measured. The "new light" in the poem 'New light on Terry Street' is the new light in which the poet sees the working classes. As in 'The Clothes Pit', the people dream of distant horizons — in this case the children dream of "sand, and the sea which they have not seen" — whereas the details of the poem suggest the confinement in which most of them live: young mothers sitting only outside their houses; the "inches" of the pavement; the window ledges on which the radios are placed. There is activity in the poem, but the activities seem like gestures, like the prowling of caged animals: mothers chew gum, knit or push prams to-and-fro, while children bounce balls or pedal their trikes slowly within dusty hollows. The opening image is of confinement — the poem begins with the clutter and claustrophobia of a child's playroom on wet days — and the final images are of waste, lost opportunity and of people having grown too old, too lethargic and too complacent to bring about change in their lives.

Images of waste, dust, erosion and time pervade the poems. In 'New Light on Terry Street', children "pedal their trikes slowly through dust in hollows"; in 'Incident in the Shop' "winter bulbs / Die of thirst, in the grip of a wild dust"; in 'A Window Affair', the poet's life stares out of a window through "thin shifts of dust on the sunning glass". Often dust is juxtaposed with images of life such as the children on the trikes, the bulbs and the sun.

This unfulfilled potential is highlighted in many of the poems by the images of our consumer society's waste. In 'The Clothes Pit', for example, we have "the litter" of pop music; while 'Sunday Morning Among the Houses of Terry Street' opens with images of fag-packets, "balls of fish and chip newspaper" and "wet confectionery wrappers becoming paste, / Things doing nothing, ending, rejected". They also reinforce a widespread malaise which is of a sexual and sensual nature. In 'The Clothes Pit', the new working class gets "sick" (not just drunk) on "cheap Spanish Burgundy", while in 'After Closing Time', the "street tarts" are "the agents of rot".

These images betray aspects of working-class life that, despite his own origins, repel the poet and yet interest him. There is an unrelenting interest in physical failings: the old men in 'The Patricians' suppress "coughs and stiffnesses"; young women in 'The Clothes Pit' end up looking "fat and unlovely"; the wife in 'Incident in the Shop' is attractive, but "unstylized". 'Sunday Morning Among the Houses of Terry Street' particularly betrays the natural repugnance which Dunn admitted to John Haffenden: how for some years he did have "an active dislike of Terry Street itself and all streets like it, and especially the kind of society which allowed such streets to exist."[8]

For Dunn, as for Anne Stevenson, however, the working-class men sometimes have an heroic status deriving from their work, their tenacity and their male camaraderie: they become "a pantheon of boots and overalls". And, as in Anne Stevenson's case, the poet as an observer is distanced from them. Unlike Stevenson, however, Dunn immediately juxtaposes the myth with the reality. The sense of waste, of unrealised opportunity, in this working-class environment underpins most of the poems. As in Harrison's sequence, manual labour takes its toll on the working-class men. Their work drains them — mentally and physically — so that they are unable to participate fully in family life. Dunn reminds us, at the beginning of 'Men of Terry Street', how the men leave home for work in the early morning and return only at night, in a line structured to reflect the repetitiveness of their lives. The two extremes of early morning and night are paralleled later in the way in which the men are either too sad or too jovial. Their work and the relentless rhythm of their lives rob them not only of the day, but of mundane emotions.

In his sympathy for those who are unfulfilled, Dunn comes closer than usual to the working-class characters of his poetry and often the more distanced perspective from which he otherwise tends to judge them is momentarily abandoned. 'Incident in the Shop' alternates between these perspectives. In the first two lines of the poem, Dunn is once again at a distance from his subject, appreciating the female customer's unstylized good looks, but noticing in a slightly denigrating way that "she wears no stockings, or uses cosmetics". When, in the next two lines, he suggests that she is unfulfilled, the language, abjuring the earlier reservations, becomes more sensual: "I sense beneath her blouse / The slow expanse of unheld breasts." The poet moves out of himself, as it were, into a vicarious awareness of how she feels: "I feel the draughts on her legs, / The nip of cheap detergent on her hands." Suddenly, the poem moves to an imagistic summary of her condition which in plainer language might have appeared simplistic, condescending or even cruel: "Under her bed, forgotten winter bulbs / Die of thirst, in the grip of a wild dust." The fact that the bulbs are under her bed associates them with her sexuality. The sense of death and neglect in the first part of these lines stands in sharp contrast to the sensual violence of "grip" and "wild". After this image, the voice of the poem changes again, once more introducing a cruel aspect of her life in a matter-of-fact way: "Her husband beats her."

The last part of the poem contrasts the old gossips' rather vindictive interest in her domestic life with the poet's own sympathy for the woman. In the last two lines, the poet returns to a voice that is both sympathetic and sensual: "She buys the darkest rose I ever saw / And tucks its stem into her plastic belt." Traditionally, this flower is associated with love, but the darkness of the rose here reflects both the depth of her unhappiness and the extent of her unfulfilment. The poem closes with a succinct juxtaposition of the rose and the incondite plastic belt in to which it is tucked.

Throughout *Terry Street*, there is a tension between a realistic, often disillusioned, documentary voice and a poetic imagination which promises, at least for a while, to transform this reality. Dunn attributed the way in which the realism in his work is invariably at odds with other tendencies to his Scottish origins: "As a Scots writer I've always been aware of the possibility of lapsing into sentimentality... And the rest of the time, perhaps most of the time, I'm fighting against it."[8] He does not do himself justice, though, in suggesting that the realism of his work is opposed only to sentimentality. For the most part, it is the poetic and the realistic that are in tension.

This tension is resolved in several of the poems in favour of the transformation of reality by the poetic. For example, in 'On Roofs of Terry Street', being above the street and above the community signifies the imaginative transcendence achieved in the poem itself. The first two lines encapsulate the movement of the poem as a whole: "Television aerials, Chinese characters / In the lower sky, wave gently in the smoke." No sooner does the poem open in a down-to-earth documentary voice than it becomes more poetic, envisaging the aerials as "Chinese characters".

At two points in 'Young Women in Rollers', Dunn adopts a sympathetic posture towards the women who sit around waiting for their hair to set beneath thin scarves and who walk about in last year's fashions, "stockingless, in coats and old shoes." First, they have the grace to blush as they pass in the street. Secondly, while their bare legs would appear to signify their poverty, both culturally and materially, the poem also takes a different perspective:

> They look strong, white-legged creatures
> With nothing to do but talk of what it is to love
> And sing words softly to the new tunes

Here the image of the stockingless legs is transformed by the epithet "strong" and the noun "creatures". The women suddenly become desirable, elusive and mysterious. The boredom of their lives — they have nothing to do but talk of love and sing the words of the latest pop tunes — is lightened by the word "softly" and by the fact that they talk not of sex and relationships as such, but "of what it is to love". Later in the poem, they become momentarily transcendental, pure and ethereal:

> The movements they imagine go with minuet
> Stay patterned on the air. I can see soot,
> It floats. The whiteness of their legs has changed
> Into something that floats, become like cloth.

Unfortunately, the poetic is only marginally successful in this poem in transforming and transcending the realistic. The tension here is between "dream" and "ideal", on the one hand, and knowledge of their real lives, on the other. It is difficult for Dunn to accept them on their own terms. Eventually, the poem regresses to the realism of their world: "Tonight, when their hair is ready, after tea, / They'll slip through laws and the legs of policemen." The women have now become less pure and less ideal, but also less insubstantial. The incondite "reality" of their lives — hair-dos, tea, avoiding policemen and the law — rushes back. The phrase through "the legs of policemen" is deliberately ambiguous referring not only to the way the women have to give the police the slip, but also to the sexuality of their lives. In the penultimate line, the poet admits: "I won't be there, I'll be reading books elsewhere."

In 'A Window Affair', the window is a border where the poetic, the ideal, and realism coalesce. The poem centres on the poet's view of a woman through a window:

> Her window caught the winter sun and shone.
> I imagined everything, the undressing, love,
> The coy sleep. But there was nothing to say.

The "winter sun", caught by the window, signifies the poetic, transforming power of the imagination and the word "shone" suggests what is imaginatively transformed. But, as in 'Young Women in Rollers', realism soon intrudes and reasserts itself:

> Untouchable,
> She was far away, in a world of foul language,
> Two children, the television set in the corner,
> As common as floral wallpaper or tea,
> Her husband in at six to feed the greyhounds.

142

The poem charts the poet's increasing disillusionment: "The goodwill became full of holes like a sieve. / I grasp only the hard things, windows, contempt."

In 'A Removal from Terry Street', one of the few poems written from the perspective of an inhabitant of Terry Street, Dunn seems to be deliberately trying to restrain himself from focusing upon what he describes in 'A Window Affair' as "the hard things, windows, contempt":

> On a squeaking cart, they push the usual stuff,
> A mattress, bed ends, cups, carpets, chairs,
> Four paperback westerns.

The derogatory connotations of the word "stuff" is reinforced by the way in which our attention is drawn to the absence of anything cultural other than "Four paperback Westerns". Yet all of this criticism is overturned by a half joke at the end of the poem which actually furnishes an image of the frustration of living in this urban environment:

> There is no grass in Terry Street. The worms
> Come up cracks in the concrete yards in moonlight.
> That man, I wish him well. I wish him grass.

Dunn himself has said of this poem:

> The last line of the poem is intended as ironic. That man, and his lawnmower, setting off for a new place, perhaps a better place, and perhaps some grass for him to look after, moved me; and yet I also saw this vignette as an image of vanity, of that man's touching faith in progress, and my own unjustifiable cynicism in an environment which perfectly embodied the shame and wormwood of British society.[9]

In *The Happier Life*, the tension between the poetic and the realistic poles of Dunn's imagination is suspended, rather than resolved, by the development of the tendency in *Terry Street* to catalogue and categorise as a more explicit dimension of the poetry. In this respect, *The Happier Life* anticipates *Barbarians* which Dunn explains "is 'about' psychologies of class, racial and national superiorities — distempering, recalcitrant subjects."[10] Thus, in the description of the night-time city, so obvious a subject in *Terry Street*, the poet now focuses upon *groups*

143

of people: solemn couples, fat boys, sleepy old men, seducers, bored narcissists, stylish youths and lonely drunks. In 'The Hunched', too, the focus is upon categories: sullen magnates, scholars, and children. Individuals are subordinate to the different groupings in which they are placed.

Maurice Lindsay has carped that in *The Happier Life*: "The Terry Street Room-at-the-Top Dunn becomes... Life-at-the-Top Dunn."[11] The extent to which Dunn has become even more distanced from the people about whom he writes, axiomatic of this larger shift of focus, can be seen in the way in which he chooses to concentrate upon the upwardly mobile — the lower middle classes — who have parties in Edwardian houses. A comparison of 'The Worst of all Loves' in *Terry Street* with 'The Hunched' from *The Happier Life* is especially revealing.

The former declares Dunn's interest in "the people seen / In glances and longed for...." They are seen as a result of deliberately looking: "When the sleep of travelling makes us look for them." But in 'The Hunched', they steal upon the poet who becomes aware of them unwillingly: "I stooped to lace a shoe, and they all came back, / Mysterious people without names or faces."

In 'The Worst of All Loves', the effect of these people is to make the poet aware of "what great thing" he has lost. But in 'The Hunched' he declares: "And not one of them has anything at all to do with me." Most of the characters in 'The Hunched' are repulsive — displaying the kind of physical distaste, if not disgust, which we find in poems from *Terry Street*, but in a more qualified way. The magnates are "hunched into chins and overcoats"; scholars avoid "things too real"; children are "furtive with their own parts"; and the poem moves on to "a lonely glutton", "a coughing woman" and "a son's cold hand". In their different ways, they are all "hunched": some such as the overweight magnate and the old woman with "the invisible arch of death in her back" literally; others such as the scholar, the son and the glutton are metaphorically hunched in their attitude towards life. But the poet, haunted by these people, is also hunched. The way in which Dunn was attracted in *Terry Street* to the darker, seedier side of life at the same time as he was repelled by it takes a new direction in *The Happier Life*. He tries, unsuccessfully, to shut out the inhabitants of the underworld, overtly signified in 'Midweek Matinee' by "the undeserving drunks". Despite the wry humour, Dunn knows they are not to be excluded easily:

> You never answer telephones or give parties.
> If you have a sense of humour, I want to know.
> You claim the right to be miserable
> And I can't stand what you bring out into the open.

Alongside, but not axiomatic with, this increasingly overt desire to suppress, if not exclude, the gross, a new anger emerges in his work akin to that which pervades the work of Harrison and Wainwright. And as in their cases, the anger is seen as stemming from an ancestry of disinheritance:

> We shouted the bad words to their sisters,
> Threw stones at hens, blocked up the froggy drains.
> Outlaws from dark woods and quarries,
> We plundered all we envied and had not got,
> As if the disinherited from farther back
> Came to our blood like a knife to a hand.

Increasingly, and especially in *Barbarians* (1979), he focuses, like Harrison in *from 'The School of Eloquence'*, upon his own emergence into the middle class; the way in which he has bettered himself by entering through education "cultured" society. The metaphor he chooses for this is that of entering through a narrow gate in the wall which the cultured have built around themselves. The wall is protective in that it keeps out the lower classes, while allowing the upper classes to cultivate their sensibilities undisturbed. But the garden is an appropriate metaphor as a garden, cultivated and enjoyed by the upper classes, is inevitably dependent upon the labour of the working classes. Yet while Dunn has entered through the narrow gate, the energy and commitment of his work stems from his working-class roots. As in Harrison's case, Dunn is aware of how working-class speech has been denigrated by the upper classes. 'In the Grounds' attacks "those / Who when we speak proclaim us barbarous." Indeed, Dunn has said of *Barbarians* that it is "largely written in metre for the reason that someone in the *persona* of a barbarian would be expected to write them in grunts."[12] To the Greeks, a barbarian was someone who did not speak their language and whose foreign tongue was depicted derogatorily as "bar-bar, bar-bar". But more so than in Harrison's case, Dunn is angry at how, as he says in 'The Come-on', background, "takes over, blacking out what intellect / Was nursed by school or book."

The garden is similarly employed as a metaphor in Wainwright's 'The Garden Master' which, too, looks back to the fear of English aristocrats that revolution would spread across the channel from France. There, the master loses control of his garden to the gardener. This is the threat, the promise, upon which Dunn also closes 'The Come-on' and which undermines the gardener's apparent obsequiousness and imitation of upper-class aesthetics:

> One day we will leap down, into the garden,
>   And open the gate — *wide, wide.*
> We too shall be kings' sons and guardians,
>   And then there will be no wall:
> Our grudges will look quaint and terrible.

Dunn himself has explained how:

> My political convictions are substantially the same now as when I wrote *Terry Street*, but in that book they were submerged in the material of the poems.... By temperament, I'm unwilling to be a 'political poet'. There are times, though, when everyone is led to go against the grain of what they expect of themselves. My imagination has tried to encompass political feeling — I don't like it, but imagination often does what the conscious mind may not particularly want it to do.[13]

In looking upon Terry Street as an outsider, Dunn not only revaluates notions of the working class derived from his own ancestry, but achieves a deep sense of the connection between culture and class which anticipates his later work. The opening poem of *St. Kilda's Parliament* in which "the photographer revisits his picture" begins with the way in which the photograph is a cultural exploitation of the islanders. Their primitive life is captured by the camera as it will be seen by cultured viewers. But soon, the poem begins to turn this interpretation on its head. The process begins with the image of the dogs who are "doing nothing / Who seem contemptuous of my camera."

Eventually, the reader is encouraged to be as contemptuous of the camera and urged to revalue the lives of those who might be "wisemen or simpletons":

> But in that way they almost look alike
> You also see how each is individual,
> Proud of his shyness and of his small life
> On this outcast of the Hebrides
> ....

The key words here are "individual" and "proud" which undermine the anonymity, hardship and underprivilege stressed in the opening of the poem where the men all stand barefoot, "with a set half-smile" and in "files". The arduousness and poverty of their lives cannot be gainsaid. But the fact that they are hardly able to scrape a living is offset by the richness of their lives in other ways. The phrase "eyes *full* of weather and seabirds" (my italics) is important in this respect. Here the photograph is reinterpreted. The emphasis has shifted from the barefeet, the tam-o'shanters, and the half-smiles to full eyes and "how each man looks /·Secure in the love of a woman...". They might appear simpletons to cultured folk, but they have wisdom based upon knowledge of the weather, the environment and traditional crafts. In reassessing the past, this poem tries to sting the cultured classes into a revaluation of their lives: here are "those who never were contorted by / Hierarchies of cuisine and literacy." Of course, the way of life of the islanders is doomed by the march of what we call "progress", but the poem is not simply a Hardyesque treatise of the destruction of an organic community by the advance of modern society. The photograph signifies a particular, cultured, mainstream, educated view of what is deemed outside and beneath it which the poem exposes.

In *St. Kilda's Parliament*, there is a broader and more profoundly philosophical, political stance than in many of the earlier collections, but of the kind we have already identified with poets writing from positions outside the conventional parameters of cultural power. In several respects, it is epitomised in the way in which 'The Apple Tree' takes a long view of history, identifying the epochs in which much of what took place now appears reprehensible to us. In particular, the puritan cultures are singled out for criticism. But the influence of Dunn's origins in a class without power is often implicit as the poet tries to disentangle himself from repressive human constructions and to disentangle culture, as a human invention, from place. The apple tree becomes a symbol of individual growth and development away from repressive cultures in general and the intolerant kirk in particular. This possibility is described, ironically, in religious terms: "A sapling nursed to fruit impersonates salvation." It is encapsulated in the final image of the poet holding earth from the kirkyard in one hand and an apple in the other.

The broad view of history which is taken in *St. Kilda's Parliament* is the politicised perspective which we have already identified among working-class poets. In 'The Miniature Metro', the poet contemplates how a bulldozer had opened up a hillside and enabled him to see further into the earth than has previously been possible. Prior to this, he had only been able to see down to a plough blade's or drain's depth and this may be taken by the reader either literally or metaphorically. The extent of the view revealed by the bulldozer signifies the perspective which the poet tries to assume in this work. *St. Kilda's Parliament* attempts, as it were, a bulldozer's view of human history. To reinforce this metaphorical interpretation of the poem, the poet compares his association of poetry with a plough to Heaney's comparison of writing with "digging". The bulldozer is able to reach down to "strata where roots end". At this level, relics are absent and one finds only "pure mineral"; the poem taking up the central theme of 'The Apple Tree' of reaching beyond repressive cultures to a new sense of freedom.

In *St. Kilda's Parliament*, there is a clear concern, too, in common with other Northern poets of working-class ancestry, with trying to come to terms, on a profound, philosophical level, with the extremes, and especially the horrors, of human experience and of society: the horror of being blinded in war; the ruthless persecution of a young girl accused of being a witch by members of the kirk; the way in which lamp-posts have become makeshift gallows for summary executions. The attempt to try and include the opposing extremes in one coherent world-view leads to a fresh inventiveness in Dunn's poetry. Lamp-posts and paper clips are not what we might think of as ready subjects for poetry. Indeed, by calling his poem 'Ode to a Paperclip' Dunn suggests it is a mere parody. But the lamp-post becomes a symbol around which various aspects of human life, society and culture and the horror of execution are focused, while the paper clip serves as a means of probing a stratified society:

As readily as you fasten up the drafts
  A democrat compiles on human rights.
Good and/or bad, important/unimportant —
Little survivor, you go where you're sent,
On memoranda from the Chiefs of Staff
To Ministers of State, down to the note
A man finds clipped inside his wage packet,
Saying, *Sorry, you've been made redundant.*

Coins are a recurring symbol in *St. Kilda's Parliament*, focusing concerns which may be traced back to Dunn's working-class origins. In 'The Local' a man is "five pence short of what a refill costs." In 'Second-hand Clothes' "A girl annoints a dress / With four silver coins." In 'Washing the Coins', the farmer's wife pours "a dozen pennies of the realm" into the boy's cupped hands where she also places two florins. In 'Lamp-posts', the reader is advised: "Throw them a coin or two, for they are beggars / Touting beneath electric epaulettes." In 'Savings':

She'd help me shake her Twining's tin —
Half-crowns and a sovereign,
Shillings, sixpences and florins
Rattled on the paper notes.

These symbols focus the larger concerns with subservience, exploitation, inequality, betrayal and guilt. They are concerns rooted in the cultural framework in which Dunn was born and brought up and are part and parcel of the process by which a writer working at the social and geographical margins tries to find and define his/her identity. John Wilson, for example, a poet who was employed as headmaster of Greenock Grammar School on condition he give up "the profane and unprofitable art of poem-making", complains:

For the sake of my family, I waste
What once I loved, and hope to see disgraced
My living mind, which, for a stipend, closed
Itself on life....

He is angry and disgusted at himself for having to comply with the "pious dumplings": "Blame me, if you must blame me; and say my will / Was feeble-weak, and then contemptible." The young narrator of 'Washing the Coins' similarly feels the humiliation of having to comply with others reinforced by the repetition of "Until they let you stand up straight" within only the first eight lines of the poem. Of course, this line may be read literally: starting at seven in the morning, he has to bend to pick the potatoes in the wake of the digger. It may also be read metaphorically: to be allowed to stand up straight in the sense of regaining one's dignity. For one brought up in Scotland, ignominiously yoked from a nationalist's point of view to England since 1707, this becomes important on many levels. In the course of the poem, the narrator comes to feel he has "something in common" with the "bedraggled" Irish workers and to understand their "happy rancour" until, significantly, the farmer's wife cannot tell him apart from the Irish boys. The dirt washed from the coins is not only the literal dirt which clings to his hands from the fields, but guilt over his complicity in his own indignity as well as shame over generations of such servitude, which only a poet with origins in a colony or the working class can really understand, reinforced by the word "scrubbed", itself recalling Pilate or Lady Macbeth:

> My mother ran a basin of hot water.
> We bathed my wages and we scrubbed them clean.
> Once all that sediment was washed away,
> That residue of field caked on my money,
> I filled the basin to its brim with cold;
> And when the water settled I could see
> Two English kings among their drowned Britannias.

It is this poem which enables us to understand not only the significance of Green Breeks for Scott, but for Dunn himself, a significance rooted as much in Dunn's working-class as in his Scottish origins:

> Green Breeks did not inform. He kept his pride.
> He nursed his lovely grudge and sword-cracked skull
>   And took both pain and bribery in his stride.
>   They offered cash, 'smart money', to annul
> Shame and dishonoured laws. He would not sell
> His wound: let them remember it....

The interest of the poem is in the way that Scott, under encouragement of supporters such as the Countess of Sutherland, appropriated and idealised the "boy-barbarian". As in the previous poem, Dunn is interested in the processes of political domination and the way in which one culture, nation or class is legitimised in its dominance over another. Moreover, Dunn recognises, as Gwyn A. Williams suggested in relation to Wales, that concern with myth, in this case on the part of Scott and his contemporaries, often represents a retreat from the real history of the people.

Indeed, throughout *St. Kilda's Parliament*, there is a vicarious sympathy for the disadvantaged which constantly betrays Dunn's working-class ancestry. Dunn actually admits "a pretence of being a John Buchan of the underdog". In 'Washing the Coins', he challenges the reader to understand what it means to see yourself "portrayed / Among the wretched of the native earth." In 'Second-hand Clothes', he sees himself as "a suitably ashamed / Observer of the poor." 'The Local' closes with a lament:

> We could talk of life
> And death and poetry. We could be neutral,
> Smiling with goodwill. Instead, we stand
> In this armpit of English vernacular,
> Hopelesly in touch with where we are.
> The dead lie under our feet like pipelines.
> The unacknowledged, counting pennies from
> An outstretched palm, know what compassion's worth,
> Here, humbly, off a High Street in the North.

At the same time, there is anger at, and bewilderment over, those who exploit the inequalities within society. In 'Second-hand Clothes', the proprietor of the shop has not only seen the abhorrent reality of poverty, but served its enterprise. Her resilience is contrasted with the poet's own concern and virtual inability to cope with so much which he finds unpalatable: "When I got home, I crawled / Into my mouth...".

The interest in 'Second-hand Clothes' in the sense of a contract between the proprietor and those who come to buy, a contract signified by the coins on her watery tray, is also a key feature of 'Monumental Sculptor'. Again, the interest is in the proprietor's impercipience or insensitivity — in this case, signified by the "respectful smirk" on his face. The sense of complicity here is two fold: concerning the apprentices who come to assume his "likeness", especially significant given that the poem opens with "That look on his face", and also the customers who enter holding his designs with his price-list. Of course, the need to remember a loved one is the other side of the proprietor's hard-nosed, profitable business: in the office a Bible, ransacked for text, is juxtaposed with "spiked invoices". As in 'Second-hand Clothes', there is stress, too, on the unsophisticated ambience of the business premises: in the former on the flicked ash and bare boards; here on how "a kettle — boils among the stone-dust" and on the man's dusty eyebrows. In both places, there is al-most an air of neglect.

The idea of contracts of one kind or another pervades many of the poems in *St. Kilda's Parliament*. In 'Savings' a bond develops between the boy and the woman, unconsciously at first on his part, signified by the way in which she would take his hands in hers. A similarly symbolic gesture locks the young boy and the farmer's wife together in 'Washing the Coins' when she places her hands around his cupped hands as if they were "praying together". In 'Valerio', a palm cradles a crucifix where Christ still suffers and there is also the "outstretched palm" of "the local". What emerges from *St. Kilda's Parliament* is a web of con-nections, an appreciation of which reinforces the particular pol-itical dimension Dunn has in mind when he says he stands with the ghosts of his grandfathers.[14]

As Dunn's work has developed, there has been a growing, explicit attachment to Scotland, and especially to rural Scotland. But the attachment invariably betrays origins that are signifi-cantly working-class as well as Scottish. In 'Here and There' in *Northlight* (1988), Dunn answers repeated criticisms of his deci-sion to spend more time in the North. To the charge of "Provin-cial", his response is that he will "twist" his art "on-the parochial lie".

Douglas Dunn, then, is an appropriate poet with whom to close this part of the book. His concern with his own working-class ancestry is more indirect than Harrison's, but no less im-portant for that. We have argued that he is important because he is one of the first major poets to write perceptively about the changes which have occurred in working-class culture in his poetry and about the establishment of identities around new myths and signs rather than around traditional notions of class. But in doing so, Dunn is still concerned, at times implicitly, with his own orientation and definition, in the light of his origins within a mythical framework which might be described as "working class". Even Dunn's later work, reflecting the highly politicised concerns of many of the poets discussed in this study, is underpinned by positions determined by his ancestry. It betrays the abiding concern of those born and brought up at the social and geographical margins with the larger processes of cultural hegemony and with the way in which one class, social or gender group is legitimised in its power over another. Like much of Harrison's work, the poetry is rooted in the tensions between the perspectives and myths derived from his origins and the position he has ironically won for himself as a respected writer within the conventional parameters of cultural power.

CONCLUSION

Much of our most exciting poetry is being written away from the economic and cultural centre, at the geographical margins, where there is a varying, but considerable concern with the tripartite theme of ancestry, culture and identity. While the description 'regional' is sometimes applied to much of this type of work, it is often inappropriate. Northern Ireland and Wales, for example, are historically, geographically and culturally more than regions, and the best of these writers transcend the merely 'regional' and contribute to the diversity of British poetry. Yet the label 'regional', a derogatory epithet, which would not be applied so readily to writers who base their work upon, say, London, New York or Paris, exemplifies our continued reluctance to see work written away from the cultural and geographical centre as more than merely parochial.

It is not surprising, then, that there is in all these areas a concern with a specific past, a loyalty to a specific culture or subculture, and an interest in tracing continuities. Of course, writers in, say, Wales and Northern Ireland are dealing with issues of nationalism and colonisation and are trying to reclaim a cultural identity eroded, overtly and covertly, by conquest and by complicity. Yet writers working in areas such as Northern England, where working-class culture and traditions are strong, share some of the concerns of Welsh and Irish writers: a sense of enforced inferiority, the struggle against hegemonic forces that would erode and destroy their cultural identity, and the reclamation of a wealth of accumulated experience which mainstream culture would deny. And all these writers find themselves working in a language which, to varying extents, is not indigenous to the locality.

Many discussions of the past in British literature have concentrated upon the way in which writers look back to, but do not retreat upon, the past in order to move forward. A great deal of

154

attention has been paid to contrasting organic communities of the past with the seeming isolation, alienation and mechanistic nature of life in the present. Yet often the real interest of the poetry lies not in the recreation of the past, but in the dynamic between the present and the past. The intellectual breadth and depth of the poetry often derives from its awareness of cultural processes, of the forces of hegemony and of the processes by which one cultural position is legitimised in the precedence it takes over another. While many discussions of Heaney's early work, for example, have focused upon the rich, sensuous language and the prioritising of a rural, almost idyllic, Ireland, the concern with the cultural processes of legitimation and hegemony has not been done justice by the critics.

As we suggested at the outset, the linguistic and structural inventiveness in the work of many of these poets is rooted in a dynamic between author, text and reader where the reader is presumed to be an outsider who has to be drawn into an engagement not only with a particular past, but with issues arising out of the engagement. In Wales, for example, English-language poets, writing in the wake of R.S. Thomas, have often served to engage English-speaking readers in a debate about issues of culture at a level which had not been possible beforehand. Yet poetry and politics are uncomfortable bed-fellows. While campaigns for the Welsh language in Wales have excited poets and prose writers, they have tended to make political poetry seem too much like sloganising. So, the drift away from the overtly politicised poetry of the sixties in Wales, exemplified by poets such as Raymond Garlick, should not surprise us. But this does not mean that contemporary poets are less concerned than previous generations with issues of nationalism and culture, only that their involvement is more subtle. We find the issues being tackled, as in the work of Oliver Reynolds, in complex, innovative and intellectually searching ways. Welsh, English-language writers have stepped out from under the old guilt-ridden anxieties which bedevilled the Welsh, English-language intelligentsia of R.S. Thomas' generation, and have developed an aesthetic that despite the English-language in which it is written is, nonetheless, Welsh.

The existence of publishing houses in Wales devoted to publishing good work by Welsh writers in the English language has given impetus to the publication of women writers. Their work has called into question much of Welsh culture which in its national images and traditions is essentially male orientated. From the evidence of their poetry and their published statements, many poets in Wales — male and female — are finding it increasingly difficult to relate to the traditional, generic ideas of what constitutes Welsh culture whether it be the macho, mass media-bound version or the traditional, more literary notion of a rural based, Welsh-language culture. There is also a greater tendency to write from particular environments within Wales and often from the perspectives of English-language speaking, urban areas where, after all, the majority of people in Wales live.

The Welsh, English-language poets have much in common with writers from urban, industrialised areas such as those of the North of England. Among those of working-class origins there is a similar sense of being caught between classes, similar anxieties about class betrayal and disorientation, a similar desire to be true to ambitions new to the familial/ancestral line, and a similar need to settle one's place, to know where one stands, in relation to that past.

The familiar collective identities, such as provided by working-class culture, were never as heterogeneous as the myths would have us believe. But many contemporary poets of working-class origins, such as Harrison and Dunn, are concerned with the way in which the traditional, objective identities, such as class, are losing their privileged positions. Douglas Dunn's early work might lack the historical breadth of his later writings, but it provides shrewder insights than many have attained into the nature of this change and how, since the 1960's, new identities have been forged around consumer-culture and market styles.

Ultimately, in the work of the poets concerned with issues of culture and identity there is an increasing emphasis upon the transforming, cohesive power of the poetic imagination. But we have also tried to show how these poets' concerns with culture involve subtly politicised engagements with the processes of hegemony and legitimation and with the social realities of living at the margins, abjuring clichéd notions of what it means to be Welsh, Irish, Northern and/or working class. It is no coin-

CONCLUSION

cidence that so much innovative work has been, and is being, produced from areas where a wealth of historical experience has been accumulated and identities have been, and are being, reaffirmed.

NOTES

Chapter One: Politics and Myth in Wales and Ireland

1. Gareth Stedman Jones, 'History: the Poverty of Empiricism' in Robin Blackburn (ed.), *Ideology in Social Science* (London: Fontana, 1972), p.9.
2. See, Robert Wiemann, *Structure and Society in Literary History: Studies in the History and Theory of Historical Criticism* (London: Lawrence and Wishart, 1977).
3. Emyr Humphreys, *The Taliesin Tradition* (London: Black Raven Press, 1983; reprinted Bridgend: Seren Books, 1989), pp.5-6.
4. Kevin Nowlan, 'Ancient Myth and Poetry' in Joseph Ronsley (ed.), *Myth and Reality in Irish Literature* (Waterloo, Canada: Wilfrid Laurier University Press, 1977), p.11.
5. *Ibid.*
6. Prys Morgan, 'Keeping the Legends Alive' in Tony Curtis (ed.), *Wales: the Imagined Nation* (Bridgend: Poetry Wales Press, 1986), p.33.
7. Lady Augusta Gregory, *Our Irish Theatre, cit.* Ann Saddlemyer, 'Augusta Gregory, Irish Nationalist: "After all, what is wanted but a hag and a voice?" ' *Myth and Reality in Irish Literature*, p.32.
8. Humphreys, *op. cit.*, pp.227-8. See also, Jeremy Hooker, 'Resistant Voices: Five Young Anglo-Welsh Poets', *Poetry Wales*, 22 (1982), 70. This essay is reprinted in Hooker, *The Presence of the Past: Essays on Modern British and American Poetry* (Bridgend: Poetry Wales Press, 1987), pp.177-98.
9. Seamus Deane, 'The Literary Myths of the Revival: a Case for their Abandonment' *Myth and Reality in Irish Literature*, p.325.
10. *Ibid.*, pp.319, 326.
11. I am indebted here to Brandon French, *On the Verge of Revolt: Women in American Films of the Fifties* (New York: Frederick Ungar, 1978 rpt. 1983).
12. Peter Stead, 'Wales in the Movies' in *Wales: the Imagined Nation*, pp.171-72.

13. Deane, *op. cit.* p.323.
14. *Ibid.*, pp.327-8.
15. Gwyn A. Williams, *When Was Wales?* (Harmondsworth: Penguin, 1985), p.304.
16. Jeremy Hooker, 'Resistant Voices: Five Young Anglo-Welsh Poets', *Poetry Wales* 22 (1987), 71ff.
17. *Ibid.*, p.72.
18. See, also, my review of *Welsh Airs* in *The Anglo-Welsh Review*, 87 (1987), pp.105-7.
19. Morgan, *op. cit.*, p. 33.
20. Susan Butler (ed.), *Common Ground: Poets in a Welsh Landscape* (Bridgend: Poetry Wales Press, 1985), p.190.
21. R.S. Thomas, 'Llenyddiaeth Eingl-Gymreig', *Y Flam*, 11 (1952), pp.7-9. Translated by Ned Thomas in Sandra Anstey (ed.), *R.S. Thomas: Selected Prose* (Bridgend: Poetry Wales Press, 1983), p.53.
22. Williams, *op. cit.*, p.237.
23. *Ibid.*, pp.245-48.
24. *Ibid.*, p.303.
25. *Ibid.*
26. *Ibid.*, p.300 .
27. *Ibid.*, p.236.
28. Tony Bianchi, 'R.S. Thomas and His Readers', *Wales: the Imagined Nation*, p.73.
29. *Ibid.*, pp.76-7.
30. J.P. Ward, 'R.S. Thomas's Poems of Wales', *Poetry Wales*, 23 (1987), p.22.
31. *Ibid.*
32. *Ibid.*
33. Brian Morris, 'The Topography of R.S. Thomas' in Sandra Anstey (ed.), *Critical Writings on R.S. Thomas* (Bridgend: Poetry Wales Press, 1982), p.140.
34. Bianchi, *op. cit.*, p.84.
35. *Ibid.*, p.90.
36. *Ibid.*
37. *Ibid.*, pp.91-2.
38. Ward, *op. cit.*, p.20.
39. *Ibid.*, p.21.
40. Greg Hill, 'Editorial', *Anglo-Welsh Review* 82 *cit.* Bryan Aspden, 'Doctor's Papers', *Poetry Wales*, 22 (1987), p.95.
41. *Cit.* Aspden, *ibid.*
42. Hooker, pp.82-3.
43. Butler, op. cit., p. 191.
44. Edna Longley, *Poetry in the Wars* (Newcastle-upon-Tyne:

Bloodaxe Books, 1986), p.185.
45. Mike Jenkins, 'Editorial', *Poetry Wales*, 22 (1987), p.5.
46. Robert Minhinnick, 'Problem Class: Raymond Garlick and the Welsh', *Poetry Wales*, 23 (1987), p.25.
47. *Ibid.*, pp.26, 27.
48. Butler, *op. cit.*, pp.190-1.
49. Tony Curtis, 'Grafting the Sour to Sweetness: Anglo-Welsh Poetry in the last twenty-five years', in *Wales: the Imagined Nation*, p.118.
50. For basic biographical information I am indebted to Paul Ferris, *Dylan Thomas* (1977: rpt. Harmondsworth: Penguin, 1978). But see, also, Linden Peach, *The Prose Writing of Dylan Thomas* (London: Macmillan, 1988), pp.1-12.
51. Walford Davies, *Dylan Thomas* (Milton Keynes: Open University Press, 1986), pp.97 ff.
52. Mike Jenkins, 'Editorial', *Poetry Wales*, 23 (1988), p.2.
53. Jeremy Hooker, p.73.
54. Ibid.

Chapter Two: The Burden of History: Northern England, Wales and Ireland

1. Neil Astley (ed.), *Ten North-East Poets* (Newcastle-upon-Tyne: Bloodaxe Books, 1980), p.14.
2. *Ibid.*, p.15.
3. *Ibid.*, p.18.
4. *Ibid.*, p.14.
5. *Ibid.* p.18.
6. Hooker, *The Presence of the Past*, p.34.
7. I am indebted here to Jeffrey Wainwright's own account of his work on the audio cassette, *Jeffrey Wainwright* (Canto Modern Poets, 1984).
8. Butler, *op. cit.*, p.207.
9. *Ibid.*, pp.187-88.
10. Hooker, 'Resistant Voices: Five Young Anglo-Welsh Poets', p.75.
11. *Ibid.*, p.74.
12. *Ibid.*, pp.73-4.
13. Deane, *A Short History of Irish Literature*, (London: Hutchinson, 1986), pp.245-46.
14. *Ibid.*, p.243.
15. Longley, p.207.

16. Deane, *op. cit.*, p.244.
17. Longley, *op. cit.*, p.207.
18. *Ibid.*, p.208.
19. *Ibid.*, p.209.
20. *Ibid.*, p.210.
21. *Ibid.*
22. For her lengthy discussion of Paulin, see, pp.190-99.
23. Deane, p.244.
24. *Ibid.*, p.245.
25. *Ibid.* In an interview with John Haffenden, Paulin maintained: "But what I find at the moment is a real sense of how fundamentally ridiculous and contradictory it is to be an Ulster Protestant. It's a culture which could have dignity and it had it once — I mean the strain of radical Presbyterianism, free-thinking Presbyterianism, which more or less went underground after 1798. I pretty well despise official Protestant culture..." Haffenden, *op. cit.*, p.159.
26. Terry Eagleton, Review of *Fivemiletown*, *Observer*, 25 October, 1987.
27. Longley, *op. cit.*, p. 210. Longley is quoting Keith Douglas' advice to a fellow-poet during the Second World War. Keith Douglas, *Collected Poems*, ed. John Waller, G. S. Fraser and J. C. Hall (London: Faber, 1966), Notes, p.150.
28. Deane, *op. cit.*, p.246.

Chapter Three: From the Land of the Unspoken: Mapping Heaney's Course

1. Elmer Andrews, *The Poetry of Seamus Heaney* (London: Macmillan, 1988), p.22.
2. Blake Morrison, *Seamus Heaney* (London: Methuen, 1982), p.20.
3. *Ibid.*, pp.20-1.
4. *Ibid.*, p.23.
5. *Ibid.*, p.24.
6. Eileen Cahill, 'A Silent Voice: Seamus Heaney and Ulster Politics', *Critical Quarterly*, 29 (Autumn 1987), p.61.
7. Morrison, *op. cit.*, p.31.
8. *Ibid.*
9. *Ibid.*, pp.30-1.
10. Andrews, *op. cit.*, p.55.
11. *Ibid.*, p.74
12. Deane, *A Short History of Irish Literature*, p.238.

13. *Ibid.*, p.235.
14. *Ibid.*, pp.235-6.
15. Morrison, *op. cit.*, p.68.
16. *Ibid.*, p.69.
17. Colin Falck, *The New Review*, 2 (August, 1975), p.61.
18. Deane, 'The Literary Myths of the Revival: a case for their abandonment' in *op.cit.*, p.328.
19. *Ibid.*
20. Edna Longley, '*North*: "Inner Émigré" or "Artful Voyeur"?' in Tony Curtis (ed.), *The Art of Seamus Heaney* (Bridgend: Poetry Wales Press, 1982 rpt. 1985), p.83. This essay has been reprinted with some additions in Edna Longley, *Poetry in the Wars*, pp.140-69.
21. *Ibid.*, pp. 82, 81 and 77 respectively.
22. David Greene in *Myth and Reality in Irish Literature*, p.4.
23. *Ibid.*
24. Anthony Thwaite, *Poetry Today: a Critical Guide to British Poetry 1960-1984* (London: Longman, 1985), p.111.
25. Tony Curtis, 'A More Social Voice: *Field Work*', in *The Art of Seamus Heaney*, p.101.
26. *Ibid.*, p.107.
27. Longley, *Poetry in the Wars*, pp.200-01.
28. *Ibid.*, p.201.
29. *Ibid.*, p.202.
30. *Ibid.*, p.169.
31. Curtis, *op. cit.*, p.105.
32. *Ibid.*, p.115.
33. Jeremy Hooker, *Poetry of Place: Essays and Reviews 1970 - 1981* (Manchester: Carcanet Press, 1982), p.71.
34. Deane, 'The Literary Myths of the Revival: a Case for their Abandonment', *op. cit.*, pp.325-26.
35. Morrison, *op. cit.*, p.69.
36. John Haffenden, *Viewpoints: Poets in Conversation* (London: Faber, 1981), pp.60-1.
37. Longley, '*North*: "Inner Émigré" or "Artful Voyeur"?' p.76.
38. Morrison, *op. cit.*, p.63.
39. *Ibid.*
40. Andrews, *op. cit.*, p.134.
41. *Ibid.*, p.43.
42. *Ibid.*, p.44.
43. Longley, '*North*: "Inner Émigré" or "Artful Voyeur"?' p.81.
44. *Ibid.*, p.79.
45. Andrews, *op. cit.*, p.143.

46. *Ibid.*, p.144.

Chapter Four: Igniting Pent Silences: Gillian Clarke, Sally Roberts Jones and Oliver Reynolds

1. Hooker, *The Presence of the Past*, p.153.
2. *Ibid.*, p.152.
3. Butler, *op. cit.*, p.197.
4. *Ibid.*, p.196.
5. Gillian Clarke, *Selected Poems* (Manchester: Carcanet Press, 1985), p.111.
6. Hooker, 'Resistant Voices: Five Young Anglo-Welsh Poets', p.73.
7. Butler, *op. cit.*, p.196.
8. Curtis, 'Grafting the Sour to Sweetness', p.112.
9. Nicholas Jacobs, 'David Jones and the Politics of Identity', *Agenda*, David Jones Special Issue, p.68.
10. *Ibid.*, p.71.
11. *Ibid.*, p.69.
12. See, also, Seamus Deane, *A Short History of Irish Literature*, p.233.
13. Butler, *op. cit.*, p.196.
14. *Ibid.*, pp.195-6.
15. *Ibid.*, p.196.
16. Curtis, 'Grafting the Sour to Sweetness', p.113.
17. Hooker, *The Presence of the Past*, p.154.
18. Butler, *op. cit.*, p.195.
19. Deirdre Beddoe, 'Images of Welsh Women', in *Wales: the Imagined Nation*, p.227.
20. Tony Curtis, 'Grafting the Sour to Sweetness', p.102. See, also, Kenneth R. Smith, 'The Portrait Poem: Reproduction of Mothering', *Poetry Wales*, 24 (1988), pp.48-54. The essay is the first of four about Welsh women poets. The others are published in subsequent editions of *Poetry Wales*. The essay referred to here specifically contains material on Sally Roberts Jones.

Chapter Five: Them & Uz: Tony Harrison's Eloquence

1. Thwaite, *op. cit.*, p.120.
2. Alan Young, 'Weeds and White Roses: the Poetry of Tony Harrison', *Critical Quarterly*, 26 (1984), p.161.

3. David Lusted, 'To Skinheads: Images of Children and Youth in the Media', *Metro*, 64 (1984), p.14.
4. Dick Hebdige, *Subculture: the Meaning of Style* (London: Methuen, 1979), p.55.
5. Morrison, *op. cit.*, p.24.
6. Haffenden, *op. cit.*, p.63.

Chapter Six: A Politics of Being: the Poetry of Douglas Dunn

1. Haffenden, *op. cit.*, p.20.
2. *Ibid.*, p.11.
3. *Ibid.*, p.17.
4. Thwaite, *op. cit.*, p.121.
5. Haffenden, *op. cit.*, p.20.
6. P.R. King, *Nine Contemporary Poets: a Critical Introduction* (London: Methuen, 1979), p.221.
7. Haffenden, *op. cit.*, p.15.
8. *Ibid.*, p.19.
9. King, *op. cit.*, p.224.
10. *Ibid.*, p.225.
11. *Cit.* Haffenden, *op. cit.*, p.20.
12. King, *op. cit.*, p.225.
13. *Ibid.*
14. Haffenden, *op. cit.*, p.34.

THE POETS: BIOGRAPHICAL NOTES

Gillian Clarke is the author of four collections of poetry: *Snow on the Mountains* (1971); *The Sundial* (1978), *Letter from a Far Country* (1982) and *Letting in the Rumour* (1989). Her *Selected Poems* appeared in 1985. From 1976 to 1984, she was editor of *The Anglo-Welsh Review*. She is currently Chair of the English-Language Section of Yr Academi Gymreig.

Douglas Dunn's collections include *Terry Street* (1969), *The Happier Life* (1972), *Love or Nothing* (1974), *Barbarians* (1979), *St. Kilda's Parliament* (1981), *Elegies* (1985) and *Northlight* (1988). He has won the Somerset Maugham Award, the Geoffrey Faber Memorial Prize, the Hawthornden Prize, and the Whitbread Award. He was born in Inchinan, to the west of Glasgow, and qualified as a librarian, work which took him to Hull where he spent two years in Flixbro Terrace, Terry Street, from which experience he produced his first book of poems discussed in this study. He has also edited an anthology of new poetry from Hull: *A Rumoured City* (Newcastle-upon-Tyne: Bloodaxe Books, 1982) and *The Faber Book of Scottish Verse* (1992).

Tony Harrison's publications include *Earthworks* (1964), *Newcastle is Peru* (1969),*The Loiners* (1970), *from The School of Eloquence and other Poems* (1978), *Continuous: 50 Sonnets from 'The School of Eloquence'* (1981), *V* (1986) and *A Cold Coming: Gulf War Poems* (1991). *The Loiners* won the Geoffrey Faber Memorial Prize and Harrison has also been awarded a Cholmondeley Award for Poetry (1969) and a UNESCO Fellowship in poetry. He has earned a considerable reputation as a translater — including the European Poetry Translation Prize — and for dramatic verse including libretti for the Metropolitan Opera, New York; for collaborations with leading modern composers and verse texts for the National Theatre. His *Selected Poems* was published in

1984. Born in Leeds in 1937, he has taught in Northern Nigeria and Prague and has twice been Northern Arts Fellow in Poetry at the Universities of Newcastle and Durham.

Seamus Heaney's collections include *Death of a Naturalist* (1966), *Door Into the Dark* (1969), *Wintering Out* (1972), *North* (1975), *Field Work* (1979), *Station Island* (1984), *The Haw Lantern* (1987) and *Seeing Things* (1991). His *Selected Poems 1965-1975* appeared in 1980 and a new *Selected Poems* was published in 1991. His translation of *Buile Shuibhne Geilt* is rendered as *Sweeney Astray* (1983). Born in 1939, the eldest in a family of nine children, Heaney's family home is a farm at Bellaghy, County Derry, in Northern Ireland. Heaney was educated out of this background as a boarder at St. Columb's College in the city of Derry, where he went at the age of twelve, and at Queen's University, Belfast, where he read English and later became a lecturer. In 1973, he resigned his post at Queen's and moved to Ashford, County Wicklow, in the Republic of Ireland. Three years later he moved to Dublin where he was appointed head of the English Department at Carysfort Teacher Training College. In 1982, he was appointed Poet in Residence at Harvard University in Boston, Massachusetts and he is currently Professor of Poetry at Oxford University. Heaney's prose is available in *Preoccupations: Selected Prose 1968-1978* (1980) and *Government of the Tongue* (1988).

Sally Roberts Jones has published several books of poetry including *The Forgotten Country* (1977) and the collection discussed in this book, *Relative Values* (1985). She is also the author of a study of *Allen Raine* (University of Wales Press, 1978) and a bibliography *Books of Welsh Interest* (1977). In 1977, she helped found the publishing house, Alun Books, and its imprint the Barn Owl Press specialising in books for children. Sally Roberts Jones was born in London, but returned to Wales in the 1960s.

Oliver Reynolds won first prize in the Arvon Foundation International Poetry Competition in 1985 for his long poem, 'Rorschach Writing' and in the same competition a second poem of his was included in the final shortlist of six. His collections to date are *Skevington's Daughter* (1985), *The Player Queen's Wife* (1987) and *The Oslo Tram* (1991). Born in Cardiff, he was only 28 years old when Faber published his first major collection. Like Douglas Dunn, he shares an acquaintance with Hull, having studied drama at university there.

George Charlton's work has appeared in *Bananas, The Blue Lion, New Poetry 2* and *Stand* and his collection *Nightshift Workers* appeared in 1991. Born in 1950, he was born and brought up on Tyneside and has earned his living as a teacher in further education since 1973.

James Longwill's *A Man's Jacket* was published in 1977. Born in 1974 in Hartlepool, he was brought up in Middlesbrough. He has worked as a school teacher and as a W.E.A. tutor.

Robert Minhinnick's collections include *Native Ground* (1979), *Life Sentences* (1983), *The Dinosaur Park* (1985) and *The Looters* (1989). His collection of travel and environmental essays, *Watching the Fire-Eater*, appeared in 1992. Born in 1952, he has lived in Pen-y-Fai and Porthcawl in Mid Glamorgan. He is currently manager of an environmental information and resource centre in South Wales.

Paul Muldoon's collections of poetry include *New Weather* (1973), *Mules* (1977), *Why Brownlee Left* (1980), *Quoof* (1983), *Meeting the British* (1987) and *Madoc: A Mystery* (1990) He was born in 1951 in Ulster, and came to live in Collegelands, North Armagh. He was only 21 when his first collection was published. Like Heaney, he is of a Catholic family. He lives now in New York.

Tom Paulin's collections include *A State of Justice* (1977), *The Strange Museum* (1981), *Liberty Tree* (1983) and *Fivemiletown* (1987). Born in 1949, he is of Protestant origins and has lived in the North of England as well as Belfast.

Jeffrey Wainwright has published two collections of poetry: *The Important Man* (1971) and *Heart's Desire* (1978). His work has also appeared in *Poetry of the Committed Individual* (Penguin) and in *Faber Introduction 3*. His *Selected Poems* appeared in 1985 and he has translated *The Mystery of the Charity of Joan of Arc*. Born in Stoke-on-Trent in 1944, he has earned his living as a lecturer in the English Department at the University College of Wales, Aberystwyth, (where he worked alongside the poet and critic, Jeremy Hooker), at Long Island University in Brooklyn for a year, and, since 1973, at Manchester Polytechnic.

BIBLIOGRAPHY

A full bibliography would require an additional volume. I have, therefore, restricted this to the more accessible books and essays which seem to me essential. Many carry their own bibliographies.

Books

Andrews, Elmer, *The Poetry of Seamus Heaney* (London: Macmillan, 1988).

Anstey, Sandra (ed.), *Critical Writings on R.S. Thomas* (Bridgend: Poetry Wales Press, 1982; new edition, Seren Books,1992).

Anstey, Sandra (ed.), *R.S. Thomas: Selected Prose* (Bridgend: Poetry Wales Press, 1983).

Astley, Neil (ed.), *Ten North-East Poets* (Newcastle-upon-Tyne: Bloodaxe Books, 1980).

Astley, Neil (ed.), *Tony Harrison* (Newcastle-upon-Tyne: Bloodaxe Books, 1991)

Blackburn, Robin (ed.), *Ideology in Social Science* (London: Fontana, 1972).

Butler, Susan (ed.), *Common Ground: Poets in a Welsh Landscape* (Bridgend: Poetry Wales Press, 1985).

Cairns, David & Richards, Shaun (eds.), *Writing Ireland: Colonialism, Nationalism and Culture* (Manchester: Manchester University Press, 1988)

Corcoran, Neil (ed.), *The Chosen Ground: Essays on the Contemporary Poetry of Northern Ireland* (Bridgend: Seren Books, 1992).

Corcoran, Neil, *Seamus Heaney* (London: Faber, 1986).

Curtis, Tony (ed.), *The Art of Seamus Heaney* (Bridgend: Poetry Wales Pres, 1982; rpt. 1985).

Curtis, Tony (ed.), *Wales: the Imagined Nation* (Bridgend: Poetry Wales Press, 1986).

Davies, Walford, *Dylan Thomas* (Milton Keynes: Open University Press, 1986).

Deane, Seamus, *A Short History of Irish Literature* (London: Hutchinson, 1986).

Dunn, Douglas, (ed.), *Two Decades of Irish Writing* (Manchester: Carcanet Press, 1975).

Eagleton, T., Jameson, F. & Said, E., *Nationalism, Colonialism and Literature* (Minnesota; Minnesota University Press, 1990).

Easthope, Anthony & Thompson, John O. (eds.), *Contemporary Poetry Meets Modern Theory* (London: Harvester Wheatsheaf, 1991).

Haffenden, John, *Viewpoints: Poets in Conversation* (London: Faber, 1981).

Hebdige, Dick, *Subculture: the Meaning of Style* (London: Methuen, 1979).

Hirsh, Julia, *Family Photographs: Content, Meaning and Effect* (New York: O.U.P., 1981).

Hooker, Jeremy, *Poetry of Place: Essays and Reviews, 1970-1981* (Manchester, Carcanet Press, 1982).

Hooker, Jeremy, *The Presence of the Past: Essays on Modern British and American Poetry* (Bridgend: Poetry Wales Press, 1987).

Humphreys, Emyr, *The Taliesin Tradition* (London: Black Raven Press, 1983; reprinted Bridgend: Seren Books, 1989).

Hyland, Paul & Sammells (eds.), *Irish Writing: Exile and Subversion* (London: Macmillan, 1990).

King, P.R., *Nine Contemporary Poets: a Critical Introduction* (London: Methuen, 1979).

Longley, Edna, *Poetry in the Wars* (Newcastle-upon-Tyne: Bloodaxe Books, 1986).

Longley, Michael (ed.), *Causeway: the Arts in Ulster* (Belfast: Arts Council of Northern Ireland, 1971).

Meaney, Geraldine, *Sex and Nation: Women in Irish Culture and Politics* (Dublin: Attic Press, 1991).

Morrison, Blake, *Seamus Heaney* (London: Methuen, 1982).

Peach, Linden, *The Prose Writing of Dylan Thomas* (London: Macmillan, 1988).

Robinson, Alan, *Instabilities in Contemporary British Poetry* (London: Macmillan, 1988).

Ronsley, Joseph, (ed.), *Myth and Reality in Irish Literature* (Waterloo, Canada: Wilfrid Laurier University Press, 1977).

Smith, Dai, *Wales! Wales?* (London: Allen and Unwin, 1984).

Sontag, Susan, *On Photography* (1977; rpt. London: Harmondsworth, 1979).

Thwaite, Anthony, *Poetry Today: a Critical Guide to British Poetry 1960-1984* (London: Longman, 1985).

Ward, J.P., *The Poetry of R.S. Thomas* (Bridgend: Poetry Wales Press, 1987).

Wiemann, Robert, *Structure and Society in Literary History: Studies in History and Theory of Historical Criticism* (London: Lawrence and Wishart, 1977).
Williams, Gwyn A., *Madoc: the making of a myth* (London: Eyre Methuen, 1980).
Williams, Gwyn A., *The Welsh in their History* (London: Croom Helm, 1982).
Williams, Gwyn A., *When Was Wales?* (Harmondsworth: Penguin, 1985).

Articles

Bell, Ian, 'Diminished Cities? Contemporary Poetry in Wales and Scotland', 27 *Poetry Wales* (1991), pp.28-31.
Cahill, Eileen, 'A Silent Voice: Seamus Heaney and Ulster Politics', *Critical Quarterly*, 29 (Autumn, 1987), pp.55-69
Dunn, Douglas (ed.), 'Mañana is Now', *Encounter*, (Nov. 1975), pp.76-81.
Foster, John Wilson, 'The Poetry of Seamus Heaney', *Critical Quarterly*, 16 (Spring 1974), pp.35-48.
Grant, Damian, 'Verbal Events', *Critical Quarterly*, 16 (Spring 1974), pp.81-6.
Grant, Damian, 'The Voice of History in British Poetry, 1970-1984', *Études Anglaises*, 38 (1985).
Hederman, Mark Patrick, 'Seamus Heaney: the Reluctant Poet', *The Crane Bag*, 3 (1979), pp.61-70.
Longley, Edna, 'Fire and Air', *The Honest Ulsterman*, 50 (Winter, 1975), pp.179-83.
Longley, Edna, 'Stars and Horses, Pigs and Trees', *The Crane Bag*, 3 (1979), pp.54-60.
Longley, Edna, 'Heaney: Poet as Critic', *Fortnight*, (Dec. 1980), pp.15-16.
Lusted, David, 'To Skinheads: Images of Children and Youth in the Media', *Metro*, 64 (1984).
Mahon, Derek, 'Poetry in Northern Ireland', *Twentieth-Century Studies*, (Nov. 1970), pp.89-92.
Minhinnick, Robert, 'Problem Class: Raymond Garlick and the Welsh', *Poetry Wales* , 23 (1987), pp.25-28.
Peach, Linden, 'Incoming Tides: The Poetry of Gillian Clarke', *The New Welsh Review*, 1 (1988), pp.75-81.
Peach, Linden, 'Oliver Reynolds and the Welsh Language', *Poetry Wales*, 24 (1988), pp.34-37.
Peach, Linden, 'The Martian's Disciple? Irony and Wit in the

Poetry of Oliver Reynolds', *The New Welsh Review*, 2 (1989), pp.27-31.

Peach, Linden, 'Family and Inheritance: Sally Roberts Jones', *Poetry Wales*, 25 (1990), pp.40-43.

Silkin, Jon, 'Bedding the Locale', *New Blackfriars*, 54 (1973), pp.130-3.

Smith, Kenneth R., 'The Portrait Poem: Reproduction of Mothering', *Poetry Wales*, 24 (1988), pp.48-54.

Ward, J.P., 'R.S. Thomas's Poems of Wales', *Poetry Wales*, 23 (1987), pp.20-25.

Young, Alan, 'Weeds and White Roses: the Poetry of Tony Harrison', *Critical Quarterly*, 26 (1984), pp.157-63.

INDEX